Contemporary Slavery

Researching Child Domestic Servitude

C. Nana Derby

University Press of America,® Inc.
Lanham · Boulder · New York · Toronto · Plymouth, UK

Copyright © 2009 by
University Press of America,® Inc.
4501 Forbes Boulevard
Suite 200
Lanham, Maryland 20706
UPA Acquisitions Department (301) 459-3366

Estover Road
Plymouth PL6 7PY
United Kingdom

Library of Congress Control Number: 2008942361
ISBN-13: 978-0-7618-4512-6 (paperback : alk. paper)
eISBN: 978-0-7618-4513-3

To the cherished memory of my beloved father,
Francis Wallace Derby

Contents

Foreword

The work for this book began many years ago when C. Nana Derby met children who lived and worked in apparent conditions of slavery as domestic servants. The concern these encounters generated guided her research interests in college and graduate school. It focused her Ph.D. dissertation research, resulting in this book.

Many people in her position, passionately concerned about a pressing social problem in their own country, would have written an eloquent account of the situation and what could be done about it. Unfortunately, a number of readers of such an account, while moved by it, would have questioned the potential lack of objectivity coming from a person studying a serious problem in her own country and culture. Derby chose a somewhat different and more rigorous path, doing policy research to focus on the exact dimensions of the problem and using careful qualitative and quantitative research methods to understand the process and functioning of the situation these children were in and measure its dimensions. The coherence of her empirical findings and her ability to learn from them and focus her understanding of the problem make this study objective, convincing, and thus an important contribution to the literature on exploitation of children.

This book will be of great interest to many readers–I can think of four groups in particular: children's advocates and others studying the global exploitation of children will read it to understand better how rural poverty intersects with local social institutions to bind children into involuntary servitude. Research methodologists will appreciate the judicious interweaving of qualitative interviews and quantitative national survey data to provide a convincing analysis. Gender researchers will find a nuanced account of mechanisms that make young women so vulnerable to local exploitation driven by global processes. They will also be intrigued by the fact that this may be the only study of its kind that includes in its sample and analysis people from both matrilineal and patrilineal kinship systems living in otherwise similar socioeconomic circumstances. Finally, there will be many people in Derby's situation, going to graduate school in another country but wanting to do work relevant to problems in their own. They will learn from this book the importance of arming themselves with a repertoire of research skills to provide objective and convincing results.

Hugh Gladwin
Associate Professor of Sociology and Anthropology
Florida International University

Preface

This book locates the processes of children's recruitment into domestic servitude, their working conditions, and methods of remuneration in theories of slavery to answer the question of whether child domestic servants are contemporary slaves. According to the findings, elite households in Ghana exploit children from rural regions because they have taken advantage of a historical practice that allowed children to live with older members of their extended families to provide domestic services and, in return, be given the chance to receive formal education or to learn a trade.

In Chapter 1 on Introduction and Need for the Study, I provide an outline of factors that inspired me to research contemporary slavery with emphasis on child domestic servitude. The decades of the 1980s and 1990s saw an emergence of activism directed toward the elimination of child labor exploitation and contemporary slavery. Depending on the geographic focus of specific programs, one heard about children in various sectors of the manufacturing industry (specifically in carpet and bead-making factories), street children, and those who worked in sweatshops. Existing scholarship also acknowledges child labor exploitation within the household but points to a lack of in-depth studies. The literature notes several factors responsible for this. Domestic servants were excluded from mainstream research on child labor because

- they were engaged in the informal sector which lacked adequate records keeping;
- there was a tendency for child domestic servants to be mistaken for household members;
- there was a lack of motivation to enquire into the situation of child labor when it is considered an acceptable social norm;
- several societies do not consider children's labor as exploitative; and
- numerous households that exploit and abuse children's labor are not honest about it.

Therefore, what I did to distinguish this book from others on child labor exploitation was the application of methodologies that significantly helped overcome many of the factors that obstructed the inclusion of child domestics in mainstream research on child labor exploitation. Rather than using survey methods that had proved ineffective in removing the obscurity surrounding child domestics, sampling techniques and methods of data collection were qualitative and thus non-probabilistic. I used snowball sampling techniques, extensive interviews, and, in some cases, limited observations to assess Ghana's child domestics. This qualitative approach was supplemented with quantitative data that the Ghana Statistical Services made available to me.

Furthermore, I found it methodically relevant that I adopted an approach that allowed observation of the servants not as isolated individuals, but members of groups whose activities influenced their statuses and life chances. Consequently, this study investigated the roles of parents, recruiters, and employers in the creation and maintenance of domestic servitude in Ghana.

Like child domestic servants in other cultures, participants in this study worked long hours, 10 to 18 hours a day. Most of them did not receive compensation for their services, and several factors explain this: some of the servants abrogated their contracts to return to their parents for good or to be reassigned other households, others could not withstand the abuses any longer, and yet others left because their employers took longer than necessary to compensate them.

Most of the participants in this research provided vivid and chilling accounts of domestic servitude in Ghana. This practice is an integral part of household labor in urban and semi-rural Ghana. Abuses also seemed normal to some of the participants. Employers who even abused and mistreated their servants willingly talked about it. Most of the parents were not happy about their children's enrollment into domestic servitude but considered it a survival strategy that enabled them to reduce their household size and dependence. The hope that their daughters would return with enough money or other resources to start learning a trade was also functional to them.

Many relevant responses about why domestic servitude has persisted and outlived any efforts to combat child labor exploitation in Ghana are reproduced in this book. Derrick's and Ahmed's accounts of why they recruit children for domestic servitude, Akosua's description of how her family members negotiated her recruitment with her prospective employers, an Accra employer's frank description of how she denied her servant compensation for deciding to return to her hometown, and several other direct statements enhance the quality and informative nature of this qualitative research report. Additionally, the interplay of qualitative and quantitative methodologies with statistical findings that corroborate qualitative observations provided reliability for this study.

Acknowledgments

Throughout my studies at Florida International University (FIU) and Ghana's University of Cape Coast, I received much love, support and encouragement without which I might not have attained my goal of a Ph.D.; this maiden book, a product of my Ph.D. dissertation, would have been a mere dream. I am indebted to family members, friends, and, most importantly, to the faculty and staff of the two institutions of higher education where I studied. I owe much gratitude to my major professor and dissertation committee members at Florida International University: Dr. Hugh Gladwin, Dr. Lois West, Dr. Mary Levitt and Dr. Laura Ogden. In many diverse ways, they hugely enhanced my scholarly growth at FIU. I am also grateful to Professor (Emeritus) Betty Hearn Morrow, Professor (Emeritus) Barry Levine, Professor (Emeritus) Anthony Maingot, Dr. Chris Girard and Dr. Jean Rahier for their continued interest in my professional success. I also thank Dr. Mary Free for the time she devoted to edit the manuscript.

While studying in the Department of Sociology and Anthropology at FIU, my progress would have been unattainable without the assistance and friendships of Michelle Lamarre, Cristina Finlay, Arelis Lopez, Dr. Elena Sabogal, Dr. Abdy Javadzadeh, Dr. Michael Barnett, Dr. Shelby Gilbert, Dr. Charles Nunoo, Dr. Terry Tsuji, Ann Reeder Goraczko, and Michael O'Brien; I will miss you all dearly.

When I visited Ghana for this research, I was the recipient of immense assistance from my family and friends, and I express my sincerest appreciation to them all. I will always be grateful to Beatrice Mensah, Janice Oduro-Dwomoh, Andrew Gyasi-Sarkodieh, Kwarteng Ofosuhene, and Esther Mensah who accompanied me to the various communities for the lengthy interviews, and to George Gyasi-Sarkodie for the many updates he provided me while I worked on the analyses in the United States. My heartfelt thanks also go to Mrs. Mary Amadu, the Director of Ghana's Department of Social Welfare, DSP Comfort Boateng of the Women and Juvenile Unit of the Ghana Police Service (WAJU), the Director and Staff of Domestic Services Agency at Tesano, Accra, and the Director and Staff of Oman Agency at Dansoman, Accra. Much gratitude also goes to Dr. Christina Gladwin and Dr. Barbara Walker for their help. I am also thankful to the Ghana Statistical Service for granting me permission to use the data on child labor in Ghana, and to Yvonne Vermillion of Magic Graphix for the wonderful work she did with the layout.

I thank Mary Ama Aborah, my mother, for her love, support, and belief in me. I am equally grateful to Christina and Dr. Francis Wallace Derby, Dr. and

Mrs. Fred Ocansey (Department of Guidance and Counseling) and Mr. Kissa Korsah (Department of Geography) of the University of Cape Coast; Professor Dominic K. Agyeman, Dr. Victor Ametewee, the late Dr. John Addai-Sundiata, and Professor Mansah Prah, all of the Sociology and Anthropology Department of the University of Cape Coast, and Agnes Abodom-Sarkodie for their invaluable support. I also thank the faculty, staff, and students of the Department of Sociology, Social Work, and Criminal Justice at Virginia State University.

April Dawkins, Jonathan Bulley, Dr. Garth Crosby, Dr. James Gadze, and Justice and Esther Ndubah, you were the greatest family away from home. I will forever be indebted to all of you.

To my husband Francis Asubonteng and my daughter Amy (Eno), this certainly would not have been a reality without your support.

To each of these people, and to the many friends and family members whom I could not mention here for want of space, we did this together. This is to you all.

Chapter I

INTRODUCTION AND
NEED FOR THE STUDY

In October, 2002, a United States Federal grand jury indicted a Ghanaian Deputy Minister of Finance and Member of Parliament, Mrs. Grace Coleman, for the role she played in her daughter's enslavement of a 44 year-old Ghanaian woman, Margaret Owusuwaah. During court testimony, Margaret indicated that she provided various domestic services without pay for 17 months. She further stated that a $150.00 monthly payment which had been promised to her prior to her coming to the United States was never paid (US Department of Justice, 2004). Until her escape, Margaret cooked, cleaned, did the laundry, and raked leaves. She provided baby-sitting services to other families, but Barbara Coleman-Blackwell, the minister's daughter, kept the money as well as confiscate Margaret's passport. In January 2004, Ms. Blackwell was sentenced to five years in prison and will be deported to Ghana at the end of her sentence. Her African-American husband was sentenced to six months house arrest and three years probation. Officials representing the United States filed papers seeking extradition of the deputy minister and parliamentarian to the United States to be tried (US Department of Justice, 2004; Ghana Home Page, 2004).

The government of Ghana withdrew Grace Coleman's appointment subsequent to her indictment; however, the stance of US officials drew sympathy from some Ghanaians, prominent among them being the minister's colleagues in Parliament. In an interview with *The Ghanaian Chronicle*, a leading newspaper in Ghana, a highly renowned and well-respected female Member of Parliament interpreted the lawsuit as Margaret's ploy to secure a permanent stay in the United States, and that by so doing had jeopardized the image of the Deputy Minister

(*The Ghanaian Chronicle*, 2004). In this Parliamentarian's opinion, there was nothing wrong with the indicted minister's actions; all she had done was recommend Margaret to the U.S. Embassy in Ghana for a visa. Her actions, the highly respected Member of Parliament continued, would dissuade any future attempts to help people from their constituencies to travel overseas for exposure and growth (*The Ghanaian Chronicle*, 2004).

The sympathy that Ghanaian parliamentarians showed towards their indicted colleague did not come as a surprise. Although Margaret was 44 years old at the time and qualified for employment, such abuse of labor within the household was a manifestation of the existing child domestic servitude in Ghana where many children provide free domestic services under exploitative conditions.

Ghana is signatory to the Convention on the Rights of the Child (CRC). However, urban and elite households continue to rely on underprivileged children to provide free household services. The reasons why this type of labor exploitation or slavery eluded official notice formed the basis of this research. Given the number of children one observes working in the streets of Accra and newspaper reports about their abuses in some households, one would assume there has never been any government intervention in the exploitation of child labor in Ghana. On the contrary, this research revealed that much is currently being done to protect the Ghanaian children, albeit unsuccessfully.

Early in my childhood, I observed that rural Ghana was the source of this free labor. My interactions with child domestic servants gave me an insight into their level of disorientation and unhappiness. Some of the domestic servants lived with total strangers. Others lived with family members, yet even they were treated as servants rather than a part of the households.

While pursuing my bachelor's degree at Ghana's University of Cape Coast, I wondered why the exploitation of children's labor within the household continued to be a neglected issue among scholars, politicians and journalists. By the time I entered graduate school, I observed that, at the global level, activists and international non-governmental agencies had embarked on campaigns to abolish the use of children's labor in the manufacturing sector and in sweat shops. I became knowledgeable of the sexual abuses and other forms of violence some domestic servants suffered. However, the plight of the Ghanaian child domestic seemed to evade any official notice both at the scholarly and political levels. The knowledge of this seemingly forgotten category of children and the lack of extensive scholarly research on them prompted this study.

Research on child labor exploitation was not limited to but often excluded underage workers within the household set up. A number of reasons exist for this. First, they are engaged in the informal sector which lacks adequate record keeping (UNICEF, 1999). Second, there is the tendency for them to be mistaken for household members given their location within the household (UNICEF, 1999; International Labor Organization, 2001a). Third, "In societies where using children's work is not recognized as 'child labour', but as a normal feature of society, motivation to enquire into their situation is likely to be limited" (UNICEF, 1999: 3). Fourth, most people do not consider children's domestic work as hazardous or exploitative (International Labor Organization, 2001; Lange, 2000; Slater, 1997). Fifth, many households that employ and abuse children are not honest about the fact that they abuse their child workers (Slater, 1997).

Consequently, researchers find it difficult to penetrate the household setup for interviews, conduct onsite surveys, or make observations about the exploited child. The children's work in these households can be seen as a mere extension of their duties; thus under the circumstances, the concept of employment and the associated child labor exploitation are not perceived (UNICEF, 1999). The literature, therefore, lacked a description of children's domestic servitude in Ghana and an explanation of why such abuse and exploitation of children's labor outlived all attempts to eliminate child labor exploitation and slavery and as a result it is not statistically known how many girls and boys have been enslaved in domestic servitude. For those reasons, the purpose of this research was directed toward bridging the gap in the literature on child domestic servants in Ghana.

THEORETICAL FRAMEWORK

Three bodies of literature informed this research. They are some theories of household survival strategies, theories of slavery, and the literature on child labor.

Theories of Household Survival Strategies

Household refers to "the social group which resides in the same place, shares the same meals, and makes joint or coordinated decisions over resource allocation and income pooling" (Ellis, 1998: 1). Martin Verlet (2000) describes it as "a relatively stable community of permanent residents and consumers" (Verlet, 2000: 67). As a concept, household survival strategy means "every deliberate economic act by a household with the ultimate motivation to satisfy the most elementary human needs, at least on a minimal level, according to the universal social and cultural norms, and without a full social integrating character" (Meert, Mistian and Kesteloot, 1997: 173).

The multiple modes of livelihood (MML) and the microeconomic theory of utility maximization within the household (Kevane, 2004) are two interrelated models of household survival strategies that were relevant to this research. Although both theories support the role of choices rather than structures in human behavior, the MML (Owusu, 2001) theory places emphasis on individuals' response to structural changes while the utility maximization theory elaborates people's pursuit of the highest level of satisfaction given the information and possibilities that are available to them (Kevane, 2004).

In his research, *Urban Impoverishment and Multiple Modes of Survival Strategies in Ghana*, Francis Owusu (2001) employs the MML approach to discard the notion that survival strategies are primarily associated with poor rural households. He notes that Ghanaian urban residents have employed multiple modes of survival strategies in response to the country's numerous neo-liberal economic policies which have failed since the 1970s. To substantiate his point, he uses another concept; the "livelihood strategies," as a "framework to capture *all* responses to economic change including those meant to ensure survival as well as those employed to accumulate resources" (Owusu, 2001: 3).

Although the MML strategy has a long history in Ghana and Africa at large (Owusu. 2001), the impact of recent development programs (Gladwin, 1991; Donkor, 1997; Donkor, 2001; Owusu, 2001; Hormeku, 1997; Konadu-Agyemang and Takyi, 2001; Verlet, 2000), as well as the outcomes of domestic policy mismanagement, political instability, and external shocks have had urban residents combining both salaried and non-salaried sources of income as a means of survival (Owusu, 2001). As Stark (1991) further suggests, households could diversify, either deliberately or be forced to do so in response to harsh structural changes (Stark, 1991). This was particularly true for urban residents who lived on fixed incomes prior to the failed policies. Before Owusu's research, the multiple modes of livelihood were considered a means of accumulation, a strategy for rural residents (Owusu, 2001).

Owusu's conception of 'livelihood' precludes non-monetary based interactions or networks that nonetheless augment the coping strategies of both rural and urban poor as well as the accumulation purposes of salaried workers. This missing link in his definition of livelihood strategies is what Frank Ellis (1998) emphasizes. Ellis (1998) perceives a livelihood to encompass "income, both cash and in kind, as well as the social institutions (kin, family, compound, village and so on), gender relations, and property rights required to support and to sustain a given standard of living" (Ellis, 1998: 3). I hypothesized, based on these arguments, that it is through these additional means to coping with harsh economic realities that some children are recruited for domestic servitude.

The second model of household survival strategy is utility maximization. The main tenet of this theory is that when people make choices, they direct their actions toward the maximum utility that they can derive from various combinations of accessible resources. The decision that goes into the provision of education of one's children is a subject of the utility maximization process. Research shows that families or households derive differential levels of utility from the education of their children, according to the gender of the latter. Therefore, when choices are made about which child, boy or girl, will receive formal education, consideration is given to the profitability of such an investment, although the future is usually not certain (Kevane, 2004).

Nevertheless, World Bank reports on education do not point to any significant difference between the primary school enrollment of boys and girls in Africa in general or Ghana in particular (The World Bank, 2002). However, in some cases, primary enrollment of girls tends to be higher than that of boys. Beyond primary school, girls are less likely to continue their education. This under-education of girls at the higher levels, according to Michael Kevane (2004), exists because

> Parents think there is a low return to educating girls. Female graduates may not get jobs. They may earn lower wages than males. Parents may also prefer to educate boys for personal reasons. An educated girl may not respect her parents. She may refuse to marry a spouse chosen by parents. Parents may think it unseemly for a girl to be in a classroom with boys (Kevane, 2004: 146).

Other theories propose that parents prefer their daughters, rather than their sons, to drop out of school to work because they tend to be more generous than the latter (ILO, 2002c). In many cases the incomes so generated go into the education of their male siblings (UNICEF, 1999).

Relationship between Child Labor and Neo-Liberal Economic Policies

Scholars draw a link between neo-liberal economic policies and child labor exploitation and contemporary slavery (Seabrook, 2000; Verlet, 2000). Given these two theories of survival strategies (i.e. the MML and utility maximization), child labor can occur through salaried workers' attempts to diversify their sources of income in response to neo-liberal economic policies and other structural changes, or as a result of the households' attempt to increase utility from the labor of their members.

Martin Verlet (2000) illustrates the relationship between child labor and neo-liberal economic policies through his research on child workers at Nima, a suburb of Accra, Ghana. He concludes that deregulation policies entrenched particularly in Ghana's structural adjustment programs (SAP) of the 1980s and 1990s destabilized family structures in urban Ghana, stripping men of their positions as breadwinners while plunging children into street work. Structural adjustment programs required governments to undertake austere measures focused on decreasing government expenditure and wage labor through wage freezes, redundancies, and abolition of welfare (Mbembe, 2001; Meillassoux, 2000). The SAP entailed:

> Devaluation of overvalued currencies, increases in artificially low food prices and interest rates, a closer alignment of domestic prices with world prices, an emphasis on tradeables/exportables and the gradual withdrawal of restrictions on competition from abroad (trade liberalization), privatization policies (of "parastatals" or large-scale government monopolies) a decrease in government spending, wage and hiring freezes, reductions in employment in the public sector or the minimum wage, the removal of food and input subsidies and across-the-board reductions in budget deficits as ways to invigorate stagnating economies

(ECA 1989: 18-20 in Gladwin, 1999: 4).

These transformations resulted in deregulations of the labor market, social legislation, and institutional control, which led to an overall social deregulation (Verlet, 2000). Among the changes is domestic deregulation, which refers to "the break-up of family units combined with the increasing fragility and destabilization of households which has been gathering pace and becoming more serious under the impact of the policies of liberalization through structural adjustment" (Verlet 2000: 67).

Following domestic deregulations of the liberalization processes, the Ghanaian child, according to Verlet (2000), became proletarianized. He argues that male workers who were made redundant through structural adjustments became "petrified, marginalized . . ." and lost their statuses as "family protector, chief and guide" (Verlet, 2000: 68). He postulates that women assumed the role of breadwinner but noted that because their contributions were insufficient, children were drawn into the labor force. While these conclusions legitimately explain the role of women and children in the survival of their households when men cease to be the primary breadwinners, the literature confirms my observation that historically, women in Africa have almost always played immense roles in the supply of food and other vital resources for their households.

Contemporary Child Slavery

The 1926 Slavery Convention defines slavery as "the status or condition of a person over whom any or all of the powers attaching to the rights of ownership are exercised" (the 1926 Slavery Convention). In a similar definition, Orlando Patterson (1982) saw it as "the permanent, violent domination of natally alienated and generally dishonored persons" (p. 13). That commonplace idea of slavery as the ownership of people by others is emphasized in these definitions. Until its total abolition at various times and in various countries in the latter part of the 20th century, legal documentations gave credence to such ownership (Bales, 1999, 2000, Palmie, 1995). However, slavery has taken a new turn in contemporary societies. The very existence of contemporary slavery in general is being contested currently because of this difference (Van Der Anker, 2004). What we emphasize in the 21st century is not so much the ownership of humans by others, but the processes through which their labors are acquired and exploited.

Slavery is a very fluid sociological phenomenon whose structure has never ceased to alter since its inception in the 7th century BC. What we conceptualize as slavery today is markedly different from historical forms of slavery, although the victims under both types suffer dehumanization through the loss of their freewill, power, and identities. Slavery originates from the Latin word *servus,* which means "a person whose life has been spared (*servatus*) by the captor" (Archer, 1988: 267). Its emergence occurred in reaction to the onset of private ownership and improvements in technology that led to warfare and the capture of enemies (Bales, 2000). The captives were forced to work on their masters' properties and in return, their lives were spared (Meltzer, 1980; Archer, 1988). In earlier nomadic or hunter gatherer societies, captives were killed because in addition to food insufficiency, their captors had no economic need for them (Meltzer, 1980).

Kevin Bales (2000, 1999) draws a distinction between contemporary and traditional slaves. New slaves are subjected to violent control "...and held against their wills for exploitation" (Bales, 2000: 13). They are neither owned nor held permanently by their "masters," thus their perpetrators are able to avoid maintenance costs while making huge profits through violent control and exploitation of their labor. Bales characterizes them as the "disposable people" because when they become less profitable, their perpetrators get rid of them (Bales, 2000; 1999). However, the contemporary slave holder does not have the type of legal backing that traditional slave masters enjoyed. Given non-existing legal support for and documentation of contemporary slavery, they are acquired through illegal means and disposed of in a like manner.

Kathleen Barry's clarification of child slaves in pornography helps to differentiate contemporary child slaves from all others. She argues that "[if] knowledge is a requirement for consent and maturity is necessary for sexual knowledge, then the use of children in pornography is by definition forced, and therefore a form of sexual slavery" (Barry, 1984: 99). Her definition emphasizes the subject's capability to adequately understand the responsibilities associated with their assigned positions, in this case domestic servitude, and to give informed consent. Based on this perspective, I took the subjects' capability to understand and to consent to their recruitment and subsequent assignment into consideration while conceptualizing and evaluating their positions as slaves or not. This was in addition to the various positions clarified earlier.

Although writing in an era when contemporary slavery was not as pronounced as today, Barrington Moore (1967), in *Social Origins of Dictatorship and Democracy: Lord and Peasant in the Making of the Modern World,* drew attention to differential levels of labor exploitation and slavery in particular. He coins the concept of labor-repressive systems characteristic of which is a continuum of labor exploitation with slavery existing at one end on that continuum. The permanent ownership of the traditional slave, their legal transferability, and the associated loss of their position as social beings were the worst repressive treatments that traditional slaves have had to endure. The explanatory factor in this regard is dehumanization, which for the traditional slave, inarguably, occurs through permanent ownership alienating the victims from their social and natal identities. Today, dehumanization occurs through forced labor and exploitation. Numerous contemporary slaves are acquired through forced kidnapping and trafficking, while others, although initially volunteering their participation in the job in question, end up in slavery.

Moore did not consider the inaccessibility of incomes to subjects as repression. Consequently, he excluded the American family farms of the mid-nineteenth century and hired agricultural laborers from his model. He held that while there may have been the exploitation of the labor of family members, this was done by the head of the household and with minimal assistance from the outside. Because of the lack of outside interference in the exploitation of the labor of household members, he disqualified such labor use as repressive. As regards the exclusion of hired agricultural labor from his framework, Moore was of the view that they had "considerably real freedom" and so could refuse jobs or be able to move about.

What become significant, given the argument above, are the processes of alienation, which is of utmost relevance in the conceptualization of contemporary slavery. Ivan Kopytoff's (1986) article, "Cultural Biographies of Things: Commoditization as Process" likens the procedures of alienation to the commoditization of the subjects through what he refers to as their "culturally informed economic biographies." The first stage of commoditization is the capture, kidnapping, sale, or resale of the victims which leads to dehumanization (Kopytoff, 1986). The end product of the entire commoditization process is the victim's re-humanization. Kopytoff (1986) holds that when individuals become dehumanized, their original identities, such as those internalized while living with their parents and close relations, are lost and are replaced through re-humanization. For the contemporary child domestic servant, re-humanization involves "...the internalization of roles associated with their underdog slave statuses" and other expectations that come with living in other households. "The point of removal from their original households, dehumanization and re-humanization make up the different phases of their culturally informed biographies" (Derby, 2003: 20-21).

RESEARCHING CHILD DOMESTIC SERVITUDE

This research is directed at exploring children's servitude in Ghana, primarily through the qualitative research techniques. Based on the above theoretical framework, this ethnographic study of child domestic servants in Ghana sought to answer four broad questions:

- Research Question 1: What are the processes of recruitment of child domestic servants in Ghana?

- Research Question 2: What are the responsibilities of child domestic servants and in what ways do their locations within the employing households complement their efforts of multiple modes of survival strategies?

- Research Question 3: In what ways, if any, are domestic servants remunerated for the services that they render? If they are remunerated, who receives their incomes?

- Research Question 4: Considering the processes of recruitment, methods and types of remuneration, and working conditions, are Ghana's domestic servants slaves?

The quantitative analyses answered the following questions:

- Research Question 1: Does lineage significantly affect domestic servitude, relationship between child workers and their employers, and the working conditions of children?

- Research Question 2: Which combination of factors determines employee satisfaction with their working conditions?

- Research Question 3: Is there a statistical association between the domestic servant's relationship to the head of household, and how they are remunerated for the services that they provide?

- Research Question 4: What is the relationship between formal education and incidence of child domestic servitude in Ghana?

I hypothesized that

- there would be a statistical difference between domestic servants from matrilineal and patrilineal ethnic groups as far as relationships between the servants and their "employers" and their working conditions are concerned;

- relationship to the head of the household, reasons for working, method of pay, and whether or not the respondent is paid determine the level of satisfaction with their work;

- the method of remuneration for the services provided is partially determined by the servant's relationship to the head of household;

- children of school-going age would not participate in formal education if they enroll in domestic servitude.

Research, Design and Analyses

Analyses of this study are based on an exploratory study that I conducted on child domestic servants in Ghana in the summer of 2003. There were four samples. The first sample consisted of current domestic servants or older women who spent part of their childhood serving other households. The second consisted of intermediary agencies or individuals who recruit children or adults for households' employment. The third consisted of parents whose children had served or were still serving other households. The fourth sample comprised employing households. Officials from the Social Welfare Services and the Women's Ministry were also interviewed. A snowball sampling technique was used in this study. These interviews were tape-recorded, transcribed, and analyzed manually. I also used a 2001 survey which the Ghana Statistical Service administered on over 10,000 households for the quantitative analyses.

A detailed explanation of the sampling techniques, methods of data collection, and the analyses appear in Chapter Three of this book. Prior to that, Chapter Two discusses the processes of socialization of the Ghanaian child, child labor in general, and contemporary child slavery. In Chapters Four through Eight, I discuss the analyses and findings of the study. My conclusions and recommendations appear in Chapter Nine.

CHAPTER SUMMARY AND CONCLUSIONS

The factors that prompted this research are numerous. The paucity of literature on child labor in general and on domestic servants in particular was prominent among them. As Chapter Two shows, existing research on households usually mistook domestic servants to be the children of the household heads, or they were not researched at all. Given this knowledge, I geared my methodologies and sampling techniques for this research towards the penetration of the household barrier to reach child domestic servants. The limited scientific knowledge on Ghana's domestic servants made this study primarily exploratory. That notwithstanding, I located the experiences and the meanings that domestic servants attach to their working conditions and statuses in earlier definitions of traditional and contemporary slavery to answer the question of whether or not they can be categorized as slaves.

Chapter II

CHILDREN'S CHILDHOOD, RIGHTS, AND CHILD LABOR EXPLOITATION

Literature abounds on child labor exploitation (Banpasirichote, 2000), its pervasiveness (Ramanathan, 2000; Bales, 1999, 2000), and its perceived worldwide impact. Efforts within the international community to eliminate it have also been documented. Additionally, there have been scholarly efforts at theoretical explanations of its existence and the difficulties to eliminate it (Blagbrough, 1999). The international community, including the League of Nations, International Labor Organization (ILO), and United Nations (UN) have adopted and enforced many treaties that are aimed at protecting vulnerable members of society and preventing labor exploitation from degenerating into slavery. Among these are the League of Nations' Slavery Convention (1926), the 1956 Supplementary to the 1926 Slavery Convention, the Declaration on the Rights of the Child (1959), the ILO Convention 138 concerning the Minimum Age for Admission to Employment, and the UN Convention on the Rights of the Child and Convention 182 on the Elimination of Worst Forms of Child Labor. Unfortunately, these have not been successful.

Critics observe that these numerous treaties do not directly address strategies to eliminate child labor, are vague on their conceptions of childhood, and tend to be permissive of child labor exploitation. This chapter outlines child labor in general and discusses the issues raised in some relevant treaties and how critics have evaluated them.

CONCEPTUALIZING CHILDREN'S CHILDHOOD: WHEN IS A CHILD NO LONGER A CHILD?

The literature illustrates a difficulty in the conceptualization of child labor and child slavery (Gendreau, 2000; Derby, 2003). This difficulty extends to the definitions generally accorded childhood. "Childhood," for instance, may be defined as a "...time of innocence to be protected from the brutal aggression of the real world; a period of latency during which a child needs shelter while growing up until he or she is finally ready to confront reality" (Schlemmer, 2000: 4), or as any person below the age of 18 years, according to the definition of the international community and many countries. Unfortunately, these conceptions do not fit the socio-cultural demands and specific identities of a number of individual countries.

Some researchers consider the cutoff age of 18 as a Western political construct (de Waal, 2002) whose definition was based on perceived vulnerabilities of children (Landsdown, 1994). These vulnerabilities could be culture-specific. Hence the definition does not necessarily capture the existent realities in many developing countries. The implication is that such disparities could thwart efforts to protect children based on a universally defined approach to the elimination of child labor exploitation.

Political constructions of childhood derive from two types of vulnerabilities—inherent and structural (Landsdown, 1994). Children's inherent vulnerability refers to outcomes of their physical weaknesses, immaturity, and lack of knowledge and experience, which cause them to be "dependent on the adults around them" (Landsdown, 1994: 34). Structural vulnerability of children, on the other hand, "derives from historical attitudes and presumptions about the nature of childhood" which lead to their "complete lack of political and economic power and their lack of civil rights" in societies (Landsdown, 1994: 35). The impact of these vulnerabilities is further compounded by children's statuses as minorities given the cutoff age of 18. Any person, who is defined as a child, whether or not old enough to accept employment, does not enjoy civil and democratic rights (de Waal, 2002). They cannot sign contracts, have no access to money, have no voting rights, nor rights to express their opinion or have access to courts (Landsdown, 1994; Ramanathan, 2000).

This suggests that their parents exercise the right to offer their labor and to receive the wages derived from that labor (Ramanathan, 2000). This could engender the child's vulnerability to labor exploitation. As Usha Ramanathan (2000) notes, "...the labour of the child worker is perceived as an 'asset'"... and the minority statuses of children puts this asset at the disposal of persons other than the children themselves" (Ramanathan, 2000: 148). Therefore, when unfairly treated, they cannot, without an adult involvement, seek recourse through the courts of law. Unfortunately, conventions seeking to address the rights of children do not empower them to access political and civil rights. It is in view of this, according to Alex de Waal, that the United States has not acceded to the Convention on the Rights of the Child (CRC). The reason behind this is the notion that these rights are not enforceable given the above assertions (de Waal, 2002).

Both the 1959 Declaration and the CRC hold that as human beings, children must have care, protection, and grow up in loving families. The Declaration emphasizes the need for every child—irrespective of gender, nationality, race, religion, color, language and political affiliations—to "have a happy childhood and enjoy for his own good and for the good of society" the rights and freedoms that the Declaration stipulates. The child, the Declaration further specifies, has to grow up in an atmosphere of care, affection, and of moral and material security. They are to be protected against neglect, cruelty, and exploitation and trafficking. Member states are required to provide, through legislature, an atmosphere conducive to the child's protection and security. Additionally, children are entitled to free and compulsory education which will enhance their integration into and their promotion of their cultures. Furthermore, they must have "full opportunity for play and recreation, which should be directed at the same purposes as education..." Finally, the child shall not be admitted to employment until he or she attains the minimum working age.

In addition to reiterating the rights and freedoms set forth in the 1959 Declaration, the Convention on the Rights of the Child (CRC) defines the child as "a boy or girl under the age of 18" (CRC, 1989). The CRC perceives the child as a human being who, while still an individual, belongs to a family and a community and hence must be accorded "the full range of rights." It is a fundamental right of every child to enjoy an uninterrupted childhood and to fully participate in basic education until age 15, or as the laws of their respective countries allow. The Convention further establishes standards on health care and education with the child at the center-stage. The kind and extent of legal, civil, and social services necessary for the child's successful integration into society also form a major component of the CRC.

In sum, the CRC establishes a set of standards and obligations which set forth "the basic human rights for all children, everywhere, all the time: the right to survival; to develop to the fullest; to protection from harmful influences, abuse and exploitation; and to participate fully in family, cultural and social life" (CRC, 1989). As of November 2005, there had been 192 ratifications of the CRC since its adoption in 1989. This makes it the most adopted international human rights treaty in history.

The CRC stipulates that children are required to remain in school until the age of 15 which coincides with the minimum age at which children can be admitted to employment, according to the Minimum Age Convention of 1973 (C138). Earlier conventions had allowed 14-year-old children to work in industry. The 1973 convention took into consideration the right of every child to receive at least the basic education. It was anticipated that by age 15, children attending school would have completed the basic education or would be preparing to. The Minimum Age

Convention also permits employment of 13-year-old children for light work, while 18 year olds could work in hazardous jobs. Children aged 16 can work in hazardous occupations but under certain strict conditions. In less developed countries where educational facilities are insufficient, the Convention set the minimum age at 12. It remains 14 for Mauritania, Malawi, Ecuador, Colombia, the Dominican Republic, and others. Barbados, Costa Rica, Dominica, Japan, Germany, Ghana, and other countries set theirs at 15. Tunisia, the United Kingdom, Kenya, France and Brazil have their minimum working age set at 16.

In the United States, the Fair Labor Standards Act (FLSA) sets the ages at which children may work and the occupations in which they may work (Child Labor Coalition, 2005). The minimum age for non-agricultural occupations is 14 years. In such occupations, children may work a maximum of three hours on a school day and up to 18 hours in a school week. They may be allowed to work 8 hours a day and 40 hours a week when school is not in session. The hours they work must be between 7 a.m. and 7 p.m. or 9 p.m. from June 1 through Labor Day when evening hours are extended. In addition, children at any age could deliver newspapers, work in radio, TV, movie or theatrical productions, work in businesses owned by their parents, and baby-sit or perform minor chores around the home. They should not work in the mining or manufacturing industries at all (Sunoo, 2000; Child Labor Coalition, 2005).

A number of criticisms have been leveled against the international community regarding the minimum age at which children can be admitted into the work force and the age required of them to remain in school. The authorization for children to begin work at age 15, and in some cases even younger, places them at risk of labor exploitation. For example, allowing children of all ages to deliver newspapers not only makes them vulnerable to labor exploitation but also exposes them to child sex offenders and other criminals. Additionally, although children's participation in formal education could give them some opportunity to participate in the labor market, the reverse is not always true as employment might prevent them from receiving formal education. Consequently, when Convention 138 permits less developed countries to lower the minimum age due to the absence of a lack of educational infrastructure, more children become available for labor exploitation, and illiteracy rates among the peoples of these countries increases. It is against this background that Ramanathan (2000) asserts that these laws suggest to scholars and activists against child labor that nobody is really seeking to eradicate this phenomenon. As Alain Morice also puts it:

> Anyone requiring proof of the ambiguity of the laws meant to be protecting children from exploitation need look no further than their relatively feeble efficacy by comparison with their objectives, i.e. if not actually to eliminate the phenomenon, then at least to bring it under strict control. And what better undermines a law's credibility than for it to be seen to be incessantly flouted? (Morice, 2000: 196).

I notice that what the CRC and the Minimum Age Convention have done is to prohibit child labor under certain flexible terms, consequently authorizing children's work in countries where they are most vulnerable.

This problem could be compounded by the added ambiguity of the category of people referred to as "youth." Like the concept of childhood, youth is also considered a Western political construct which does not carry any well defined meaning (de Waal, 2002). Alex de Waal (2002), therefore, refers to the youth as a "... problematic, intermediary and ambivalent category, chiefly defined by what it is not: youths are not dependent children, but neither are they independent, socially responsible adults" (de Waal, 2002: 15). They are "...not typically conceived of as productive and constructive social actors, nor, as they often are in reality, as victims, but rather as potential sources of political disruption, delinquency and criminality" (de Waal, 2002: 15). We can hardly distinguish the boundaries that set the category of youth apart from any other age group.

Childhood and youth are said to not fit the realities of other non-Western cultures because existent "sequences of maturing" in these other cultures tend to differ from Western cultural environments (de Waal, 2002: 15). In some traditional African societies, the sequence of maturing for males is "child-single man/ warrior/laborer/married self-supporting adult-elder". For females, the sequence is "girl-wife-mother" (Aryee, 1997). In Western and former colonial countries, the sequence of maturing is school-employment. As de Waal notes, the incidence of high unemployment rates and advancement in schooling makes this sequence inadequately defined. After high school, people might go on to attain college degrees and to stay longer to acquire post-graduate degrees. At the end of their university education it is not a certainty that these graduates would get employment, making their statuses less defined.

While this latter pattern is true for many African countries, the interplay between traditional processes of socialization and Western sequence of maturing blurs further the definitions of childhood and youth. In traditional African cultures, children leave that category of childhood when they ascend the traditional hierarchy of economic independence (Argenti, 2002). For males in pre-colonial Africa, this meant the attainment of a level of "economic importance that would permit them to acquire wives, build their own compound and become economically viable agents" (Argenti, 2002: 125).

Furthermore, African children as well as those in most parts of the world, especially those in rural regions, do not experience exclusive childhoods characterized solely with schooling and play. It is customary for them to provide services within the household and to be involved in their families' economic activities. Children who are fortunate in such cultures to go to school must combine formal education and household chores with work on farms (Berlan, 2004) or with street work (Verlet, 2000). An estimated 95% of children living in farming households in Ghana work on farms and an unknown percentage of these combines school with this form of economic activity (Berlan, 2004).

When tradition and political constructions of childhood grant adults so much power over children while these children are not able to adequately access formal education and consequently be equipped with an understanding of legal documents protecting them, it is not very difficult to conclude that there is a marked disconnection between realities concerning children and the fight to protect them from abuses and exploitation. Therefore, in an environment where children can neither read nor confront authority when they are being forced to work, conventions that are aimed at protecting and empowering them with civil, political, and economic rights tend to be contemptible. Additionally, the traditions that emphasize a strict adherence to a pattern of socialization that instill in children the need to obey and to respect adults also impede a successful campaign against child labor exploitation (Argenti, 2002; Nukunya, 1994; Berlan, 2004).

EXPLOITATION OF CHILDREN'S LABOR

This chapter describes the difficulty of conceptualizing child labor. As suggested, the complexity in conceptualizing this phenomenon derives from disparities in socio-cultural contexts within which children work and from questionable approaches that the international community has adopted to fight the exploitation of children's labor. If some persons below the age of 18 are permitted to work, yet do not have civic and political rights, they are at high risk of exploitation. When children and families benefit from the former's work, it is very difficult to classify every child's work as labor exploitation. Nevertheless, child workers easily qualify as victims of labor exploitation. This section attempts to distinguish acceptable forms of children's work from potentially dangerous and exploitative children's labor.

It is estimated that 400 million children work around the world. About 250 million of them work under exploitative conditions (Cox, 1999). Moreover, there are approximately 27 million contemporary slaves (Bales, 2000; 1999). According to Amanda Berlan (2004), an estimated third of all Sub-Saharan African children aged 14 and under work. Nearly 70% of them work in the agricultural sector (Berlin, 2004). In Egypt, approximately 7% of the workforce is made up of children under 14 who work on cotton fields. They travel to work in overloaded trucks, some of which have been involved in fatal accidents in the past (Mikay, 1997). From Cox's estimates, there are some children who work but not under exploitative conditions. Under what circumstances, then do we define these child workers as victims of labor exploitation or contemporary child slaves?

Distinguishing between Positive and Negative Children's Labor

Lia Fukui (2000) broadly defines labor as any activity aimed directly or indirectly at helping households meet their basic needs—namely food, shelter, clothing, health, and education. It refers to "…any economic activity contributing to the production of goods and services (Mbaye and Fall, 2000). Generally, adult members of households bear the responsibility of providing labor for the household to meet basic needs. Child labor occurs when children shoulder such responsibilities (Fukui, 2000). When household income is not sufficient to meet their basic needs, the family suffers absolute poverty (Banpasirichote, 2000). Under such circumstances, the children's labor might be indispensable. In poor working class families, children contribute to their families' welfare by taking care of household chores to free up adult labor for work outside the households to generate income for their families.

Child labor, when not exploitative, could be beneficial to the child's development. That occurs if children are supervised by adult members of their households or communities. As Fukui (2000) notes, children's work around the house is a major component of informal socialization processes or apprenticeship if these tasks are done under the guidance of adults. This is in view of the fact that the working child can get skill training from their work (Fukui, 2000; ILO, 2001a; van Gennep, 1960). Some families allow their children to live in other households with the intention that they may have a better life and most likely be provided formal education, usually in the cities (Banpasirichote, 2000; Verlet, 1998; ILO, 2001a). This occurs especially where rural poverty and its lack of infrastructure relative to urban centers are more pronounced.

It is probably based on the above observations that the International Labor Organization differentiates between positive and negative children's work, while scholars like Martin Verlet (2000) draw a distinction between children's domestic work and child labor. Children's work is positive if it is considered functional and contributes to their socialization (Derby, 2003; Lange, 2000). Functional children's work enhances the welfare of their families, provides "them with skills, attitudes and experiences…" and helps "…them to be useful and productive members of society during adulthood" (International Labor Organization and Inter-Parliamentary Union, 2002: 15). This is what Verlet (2000) refers to as children's domestic work. It also corroborates Fukui's assertions.

Verlet's research on child labor in Ghana led to the differentiation between two types of children's domestic work. The first type of children's domestic work refers to those children, especially girls, who go to school and work as hawkers, street or marketplace vendors for their mothers, aunts, or elder sisters. The proceeds from their work are used to supplement their family's income (Verlet, 2000; Fukui, 2000; Banpasirichote, 2000; International Labor Organization and Inter-Parliamentary Union, 2002: 15). The second type of children's domestic labor occurs when they are sent to live with and help their grandparents on their farms in rural Ghana (Verlet, 2000).

Rites of passage encompassed in the socialization processes of some cultures further exemplify this positive, or children's domestic work. Van Gennep (1960) differentiates between physical and social rites of passage. Social rites of passage refer to ceremonies and responsibilities which come with physiological changes in girls and boys (van Gennep, 1960). In other words, they are gender-related socializations and constructed expectations that usher boys and girls into adulthood. They "…extend over a long period, depending on the intended occupation of the child. At the end of the period, it is expected that the child, who should be closer to becoming a young adult, must have learnt a trade already" (Derby, 2003: 4). Physical rites of passage, on the other hand, represent physiological changes that boys and girls experience as they go through puberty.

In the population of study, the type of training that a child receives during socialization tends to be culturally and geographically specific. Different geographic areas in Ghana specialize in different economic activities, and this has historically determined what children learn through informal socialization. Among rural Ashantis and the populations of other forest areas in Ghana, for example, boys and girls learn gender-related farming skills before they become adults. Girls are taught how to use the hoe to clear weeds from farms, to gather forage or uproot tubers, while boys focus on clearing the land for farming. Back at home, both boys and girls fetch water from the streams and rivers. The girl's day will not end there; she will continue running errands to assist her mother in preparation of the evening meal and to clean up afterward. The boys will spend time interacting with male adults of their households.

Negative children's work, on the other hand, is synonymous with what Verlet and other scholars generally define as "child labor." It is the exploitation of children's labor which the Anti-Slavery Society defines as:

> …the employment of children in conditions which, taken together and viewed in the context of the social and economic background of the region, are likely to be harmful to their mental, physical or moral and eventually to the development of their potential (Sawyer, 1988: 13).

Whereas the distinction between negative and positive children's work sensitizes scholars to socio-cultural contexts surrounding children's employment, that differentiation tends to be inadequate in helping scholars to conceptualize the overall impact of the exploitation of children's labor. As I observed in another project, a large number of children whose work qualifies as child labor usually work under slavery conditions (Derby, 2003).

Many exploited children are obtained through trafficking. From Benin, children are trafficked into Nigeria, Ghana, and the Gabon for exploitation on farms (US State Department, 2001). From Ghana, children are trafficked for farm labor in the Côte d'Ivoire, Togo, and Nigeria (US State Department, 2001). In Asia, children are trafficked internally in India or to other Asian and Middle Eastern countries. Nepalese and Bangladeshi children end up in India through trafficking (US State Department, 2001). Some victims of trafficking end up in domestic servitude. There have been newspaper reports of their abusive experiences. David France (2000), for instance, reports of a Cameroonian girl who worked 16 hours a day for over four years without pay in the United States. Prior to sending her to the United States, her employers promised to send her to school, but this would not occur until she was freed and rehabilitated after four years.

In India, child labor victims are employed in the manufacturing of beedi (cigarette), matches, fireworks and explosives, glass and carpets, and in glass polishing, brassware making, and mining industries. Working children in agriculture are at risk of being injured by metals that accidentally drop down, machete and sharp knife injuries, inhalation of dangerous chemicals including pesticides and acids (Burra, 1995; Mishra, 2000; Mikay, 1997; Sudarsan and Raghavan, 2001; Tucker and Ganesan,1997). Some children traveling to the fields of Egypt on overloaded trucks have lost their lives through motor accidents (Mikay, 1997). In the lock-making factories of India, child workers inhale emery powder, toxic substances, and metal dust. From bead rolling to glass polishing, underage child slaves in India suffer many respiratory diseases (Mishra, 2000).

Children are also exploited in the sex industry. Sexual exploitation is defined in this context as "a practice by which women are sexually subjugated through abuse of women's sexuality and or violation of physical integrity as a means of achieving power and domination including gratification, financial gain..." (Doezema 1998: 35). When organized, it "is a highly profitable business that merchandises women's bodies to brothels and harems around the world" (Barry, 1984: 39). When practiced individually, "it is carried out by pimps whose lifestyle and expensive habits are supported by one or two women whom they brutally force to sell their bodies for his profit" (Barry, 1984: 39).

Research shows that childhood traumas, kidnapping, and control by organized criminals lead some children and women into prostitution (Barry, 1984). In the film *The Day My God Died*, children, some of whom were only 7 years old, were kidnapped, drugged, and trafficked from neighboring towns and villages into Bombay, India, where they were auctioned for prostitution at a slave-trading market. In another documentary, *Sacrifice* by Ellen Bruno, the children whose ages were not disclosed but looked younger than ten, were trafficked from Burma to Thailand and forced into sexual slavery. Existing literature further indicates that there are approximately 200,000 child prostitutes in Thailand; 60,000 in the Philippines, 250,000 in Brazil, and over 200,000 in the United States (Lukas, 1996). Most of these children suffer other physical abuses when they refuse to sleep with clients of the brothels.

From above, we observe that child labor exploitation takes various forms under different circumstances in many countries around the world. Exploitation of children's labor occurs in manufacturing sectors, in prostitution, and within the household. Children's minority status increases their vulnerability to labor exploitation in all cases. As pointed out earlier, if children cannot sign contracts or open bank accounts but are allowed to work under certain terms, their parents and other adult members of their families are privileged to sign the minors to work under exploitative circumstances. Such working children may not be fortunate enough to be the beneficiaries of the proceeds from their labor.

Child Domestic Servitude

Child domestics are known in Haiti as *restavecs* (i.e. "staying with") and *vidomegon* in Benin (International Labor Organization, 2001a). Until the 1980s, Ghanaians referred to the child domestic as "*abaawa*," which means servant. This name was replaced with others like maid, house-help, house-girls, or maidservants because *abaawa* was considered derogatory. ILO defines child domestic labor as "children working in an employer's house with or without a wage" (International Labor Organization, 2001a: 2; 2001b: vi). In the M.A. thesis, *The Other Side of the Kitchen Door: Domestic Service in Lima, Peru*, Elena Bee (1998) defines domestic services as "the many and varied types of work required to complete those duties pertaining to the maintenance, functioning, and day-to-day running of the household, particularly when performed by employed labor" (Bee, 1998: 1).

A distinction exists between domestic workers and domestic slaves. This distinction is based on the worker's age, number of hours worked, method of remuneration, and if the pay is commensurate with the services provided (Derby, 2003). The domestic worker is a legitimate worker who is mature enough to understand the conditions of her employment, old enough to enter into contracts with their employers, and can seek recourse through the law courts if unduly mistreated by their employers. Moreover, domestic workers exercise control over the ultimate decision to remain a service provider in the specific household (Derby, 2003).

Using earlier conceptions of slavery in general and contemporary child slaves in particular, I conceptualize the child domestic slave as one who suffers dehumanization through the loss of identity and freedom, works long hours without pay, and is always disposable. Although many child domestic workers easily qualify as slaves, adult migrants are reported to work under slavery conditions as well. Like child slaves, migrant domestic workers work long hours, do not have control over themselves, and are subjected to sexual abuses (Anderson, 2004).

The literature identifies two sources of recruitment in child domestic servitude: formal and informal. The first comprises of siblings or friends who are already working as domestic servants (UNICEF, 1999) and other relatives and friends who might not be working as domestic servants. They are usually free. The second source includes formal employment agencies that charge a fee for their services (Bee, 1998). Not all informal sources of recruitment are free though. As Bodo Ravololomanga and Bernard Schlemmer (2000) observe, parents whose children are recruited into domestic servitude in parts of Madagascar, as a rule, receive a certain sum of money when the child leaves home, after which neither the children nor their employers are obligated to pay these parents.

In Peru, although households have the option of using formal intermediaries or acquaintances, friends or maidservants of friends, they usually prefer getting their domestic servants through informal sources in order to avoid recruitment fees (Bee, 1998). A good number (46%) of boys and girls who work as domestic servants in Kathmandu, Nepal, are recruited through their relatives, while 16% of them are enrolled by their parents (ILO, 2001b). Employers recruit nearly 24% of these child domestic servants. Friends recruit nearly 3% of them; brokers (agents) recruit .3% while a little over 3% look for households themselves. According to this report, villagers recruit nearly 8% of the child domestic servants in Kathmandu. This report did not explain the relationship between the victims and these villages and the role they play in the recruitment of the children.

Research shows that child domestics usually live in their employers' homes and work 10-18 hours a day, usually throughout the week and often without pay (SLIMG, 1997; UNICEF 1999; United Nation's Commission on Human Rights, 2002). Their day begins around 5 a.m. (Kimaryo and Pouwels, 1999). Their responsibilities include cleaning, laundry, food preparation, cooking, shopping, and looking after young children (Shoishab, 1997). They mostly qualify as contemporary slaves.

Given the paucity of research on child domestic workers or slaves, it is not statistically known how many girls and boys have been enslaved. Recent research estimates that Haiti has about 250,000 domestic slaves (Cadet, 1998; UNICEF, 1999); Dhaka, Bangladesh, has about 300,000 child domestics; and Jakarta, the capital of Indonesia, has about 700,000. An estimated 150,000 child domestics live in Lima, Peru, and 766,000 in the Philippines (UNICEF 1999; United Nations Commission on Human Rights, 2002). It is estimated that 90% of domestic workers around the world are girls (UNICEF 1999; United Nations Commission on Human Rights, 2002).

Almost every country where UNICEF conducted research on child domestic slaves has a cultural reason for the dominance of girls in household servitude. Girls are more likely to be deployed into domestic servitude because some cultures hold that they would end up as housewives and so do not encourage their education (Mikay, 1997; UNICEF, 1999) and also because families consider their daughters to be thriftier and more appropriate to work outside the family to make money to support them (International Labor Organization and Inter-Parliamentary Union; 2002). This belief is based on the notion that girls neither smoke nor drink. In Togo, where 95% of the child domestic servants are girls, it is considered strategic to use the girls' income to support the education of their brothers. In Bangladesh, restricting the girls to household chores is considered a means of protecting them; while in Nepal, girls are preferred to boys in domestic servitude because they are considered more submissive and are less likely to run away (UNICEF, 1999).

According to UNICEF (1999), children between 10 and 14 years make up 80% of all girls who work as domestics. In many countries, domestic servants are younger than 10 years old. In Dhaka, Bangladesh, 20% of the domestic workers are aged between 5 and 10. In Togo, 16% of domestic 'workers' are 10 years or less; 50% of them are under 14, and 65% under 15. Approximately 34% of the domestic servants in Uruguay started work before they were 14 years, while in Venezuela, 25% of them are under 10 (UNICEF, 1999). Research shows that employers are more attracted to younger domestic servants because they are easily controlled and less expensive (ILO, 2001b).

Most of the domestic servants that UNICEF and ILO researched were either never enrolled in school or were dropouts. According to ILO, this is due to the fact that the majority of them are taken from their parents at very young ages. Studies on Nepalese child domestic slaves found that 18% of them could neither read nor write; an estimated 10% of them could only write their names, while a little over 53% had received primary education. Nearly 18% were educated beyond the primary school and only .3 percent of the entire sample had some secondary education.

While in servitude, child domestics suffer physical and sexual abuses. An estimated 60% of Peruvian men who grew in households with child domestic servants confessed to having had their first sexual encounters with the latter (United Nations Commission on Human Rights, 2002, UNICEF, 1999; Bee, 1998). In Fiji, 80% of the domestic workers are sexually abused (United Nations Commission on Human Rights, 2002). Ethiopian women and girls who are trafficked into Lebanon and Bahrain to work as domestic servants are reportedly raped and physically abused under debt-bondage (International Organization for Migration, 2000).

EFFORTS TO COMBAT CHILD LABOR EXPLOITATION

There have been many local and international efforts to combat child labor exploitation. These efforts entail the adoption and ratification of international conventions that are enforced to protect women and children. Adopting and ratifying such conventions usually constitute the first steps on the part of a country to fight against the targeted form of exploitation. Although countries that sign and ratify international conventions must conform to the standards and requirements stipulated within them, legislature in individual countries has failed to advance the eradication of child labor exploitation and slavery to a significant degree. While the international community has successfully created awareness among governments about relevant treaties, there still needs a lot more to be done with grassroots' understanding of the extent of the phenomenon and existing laws.

Earlier in this chapter, some relevant conventions on the rights and protection of the child were cited. I examined the 1959 Declaration and the 1989 Convention on the Rights of the Child in regard to the ways they conflicted with the Minimum Age Convention of 1973. Nevertheless, ILO continues to enforce new conventions and to embark on revised strategies to aid in the pursuit of the elimination of child labor exploitation and slavery. Between 1995 and 2000, ILO adopted eight fundamental conventions. These are the forced labor conventions (Nos. 29 and 105), the freedom of association and collective bargaining conventions (Nos. 87 and 98), the non-discrimination conventions (Nos. 100 and 111), and the minimum age convention (No. 138). The most recent fundamental convention, convention No.182, focuses on the elimination of the worst forms of child labor exploitation.

The Convention on the Worst Forms of Child Labor 1999 (#182) transcends all other treaties by focusing specifically on the worst forms of child labor exploitation. First adopted in 1999, Convention 182 came into force in November, 2000. The main goal of C182 is to bring to light the worst forms of child labor and to set the stage for their elimination. This convention observes children's vulnerability as the cause of persistent child labor exploitation and abuses in some societies. It recognizes, further, that the problem of child labor exploitation can only be solved on a long-term basis in some societies given the socio-economic and cultural backgrounds surrounding such exploitation. In accordance with these observations, worst forms of child labor were defined in Article 2 as

- all forms of slavery or practices similar to slavery, such as the sale and trafficking of children, debt bondage and serfdom and forced or compulsory labor, including forced or compulsory recruitment of children for use in armed conflict;
- the use, procuring or offering of a child for prostitution, for the production of pornography or for pornographic performances;
- the use, procuring or offering of a child for illicit activities, in particular for the production and trafficking of drugs as defined in the relevant international treaties;
- work which, by its nature or the circumstances in which it is carried out, is likely to harm the health, safety or morals of children.

In order to achieve its main goal of eliminating the above forms of child labor, the convention called on member states to design and implement programs of action to eliminate the worst forms of child labor. States were mandated to take effective steps to prevent the employment of children in the worst forms of child labor, provide the necessary and direct assistance to liberate and rehabilitate exploited children, ensure access to free basic education, and provide vocational training to liberated children.

In furtherance to Convention 182, the ILO launched a guide, the International Program for the Elimination of Child Labor (IPEC) for parliamentarians in 1992. IPEC aims at working towards the progressive elimination of child labor by strengthening national capacities to address child labor problems, and by creating a worldwide movement to combat it. Primarily, IPEC targets bonded child workers, children who work under hazardous conditions and "children who are particularly vulnerable, i.e. very young working children (below 12 years of age), and working girls." IPEC works in cooperation and in partnership with governments, educational institutions, as well as employers and workers organizations. Its actions are based on a phased and multi-sectored strategy that consists of

- Motivating a broad alliance of partners to acknowledge and act against child labor;
- Carrying out a situational analysis to find out about child labor problems in a country;
- Assisting with developing and implementing national policies on child labor problems;
- Strengthening existing organizations and setting up institutional mechanisms;
- Creating awareness on the problem nationwide, in communities and workplaces;
- Promoting the development and application of protective legislation;
- Supporting direct action with (potential) child workers for demonstration purposes;
- Replicating and expanding successful projects into the programs of partners; and
- Mainstreaming child labor issues into socio-economic policies programs and budgets.

A progress report on IPEC activities between 2000 and 2001 indicates that these steps and the main objective of IPEC contribute immensely to major strategic goals of ILO. These are the promotion and realization of standards and fundamental principles and rights at work, the creation of opportunities for decent employment and income, the enhancement of coverage and effectiveness of social protection for all and the strengthening of tripartism and social development. This report further established a link between poverty and child labor exploitation. It is now known that a vicious cycle is in operation. Child labor hinders economic development and perpetuates poverty by keeping the children of the poor out of school and limiting their prospects for upward social mobility. In addition, this progress report asserts that child labor remains a major problem of child exploitation and abuse, thus depriving many children of education and health. It said most of the child victims are engaged in the worst forms of child labor abuse, slavery being mentioned as well as bonded labor, commercial sexual exploitation, armed conflict, and domestic labor.

Ghana has ratified 46 International Labor Conventions. The first Convention that it ratified is C1, the Hours of Work (Industry) Convention, 1919. This it did on June 19, 1973, around the same time that the Minimum Age Convention came into force. Among other things, C1 requires a maximum of eight working hours a day, and up to 48 hours a week. Clearly missing on the list of Conventions that Ghana has ratified is the Minimum Age Convention. That notwithstanding, the minimum age for admission to employment in Ghana has been set at 15 years. A policy of Free Compulsory Universal Basic Education (FCUBE), which will be discussed in detail in Chapter Seven, has also been implemented, all in the effort to combat the exploitation of children's labor. The most recent Convention it ratified is C182, Worst Forms of Child Labor Convention 1999. Following the IPEC guide to this Convention, Ghana has embarked on a number of research and campaign to further its fight against the employment and exploitation of children's labor. The enforcement of the Children's Act of 1998 (Act 560) and the creation of Women and Juvenile Unit of the Ghana Police (WAJU) are prominent among such efforts.

In line with the CRC, Ghana's Act 560 promotes the interests of children and most importantly prohibits the deprivation of children's right to live with their own parents and to grow up in a caring and peaceful environment. Part V (Sections 87-104) of the Children's Act (1998) further provides legal guidelines for children's employment in Ghana. This Act sets the minimum working age at 15 (but set at 13 for light work) and prohibits the employment of children (which the act defines as all persons below 18 years) in exploitative labor and at night. Exploitation in this context refers to engagement of children in activities that deny them health, education and development. This act prohibits the employment of children in all forms of hazardous occupations. Hazardous work includes going to sea, mining and quarrying, porterage of heavy loads, manufacturing industries where chemicals are produced or used, work in places where machines are used and in bars, hotels and places of entertainment where a person may be exposed to immoral behavior. Officials of District Assemblies and the Social Welfare and Community Development Departments of District Assemblies are responsible for ensuring compliance with these regulations.

District Superintendent of Police (DSP) Comfort Boateng, a Regional Head of the Women and Juvenile Unit of the Ghana Police (WAJU) indicated in my interview with her that this organization was established in 1998 in response to calls by the National Commission on Women and Development (NCWD), the African Women Lawyers Association (AWLA), UNICEF, International Federation of Women Lawyers (FIDA), and the Association of Market Women among other organizations to provide an avenue for solving and ending problems of sexual and physical abuses of women and children by men. WAJU is responsible for

- investigating all female and child related offences;
- handling cases of domestic violence, child abuse, juvenile offense and child delinquency;
- prosecuting all such cases where necessary; and
- any other functions as may be directed by the Inspector General of Police.

Cases reported to WAJU include defilement, rape, incest, abduction, assault/ wife battery, child trafficking, and "unnatural carnal knowledge," DSP Boateng stated in her interview. When asked what percentage of the reports that the Unit receives involve abuses of child domestic servants, she stated that

> You know normally when a child is abused; sometimes it's by the help of an adult that the case is reported. In the case of the maidservant, unless people around the vicinity or the community or somebody we can call a patriotic person or some informant or somebody, a concerned person…they are the people who assist these, the maidservants or people to report cases, because the masters or mistress themselves…are sometimes the abusers, and they will not bother to come to the police station to report their own selves. They don't come in, unless they are assisted by outsiders.

While in Ghana, I saw many educational flyers or posters on WAJU. I also learned from the DSP that they had embarked on educational campaigns through television and radio. At the premises of WAJU, there were many people who had brought cases of rape or other domestic violence when I went there to interview DSP Boateng. Therefore, I would assume that many of these children are aware of the enormous help that awaits them at WAJU. What then, prevents exploited children in Ghana from utilizing the assistance that WAJU offers? Are they being made aware of the principles stipulated in the Children's Act of Ghana to protect them?

Earlier, this chapter focused attention on criticisms of the CRC and the Minimum Age Convention. It is not only in that regard that efforts to eliminate child labor exploitation have come under fire. There seems to be a disconnection between governmental and non-governmental campaigns and the people most vulnerable to labor exploitation. As this research illustrates in Chapters Four through Eight, worsening conditions of poverty and the continuing deterioration living standards make it difficult for the government, its agencies, and the many non-governmental organizations currently working together to protect these children to make significant progress.

Amanda Berlan (2004) notes that intense poverty among affected victims make it difficult to make any headway in the fight against child labor exploitation. As she suggests, the manifestation of poverty in child labor "requires sustained, long-term state investment and international support to improve education, road building and telecommunication, which would stimulate economic growth and reduce endemic poverty" (Berlan, 2004: 166). When a category of children is very poor and less educated, the gap between policy, advocacy, and practice is widened.

According to Berlan, this gap was demonstrated in Accra, Ghana, where a large and important press conference was organized on June 12, 2002, to commemorate the World Day against Child Labor. There were representatives from the ILO, UNICEF, and Children in Need, Ghana (CING). She observes that the information packets that the organizers distributed to children showed a disconnection between the targets of child labor exploitation and the campaigns against this phenomenon. She makes this comment about the information pack: "I have yet to meet a child working in the rural sector in Ghana—which makes up over 70 per cent of all working children—who would be able to take any of these steps" (167).

The information packs contained the following guidelines:

- Say no to work that is harmful and degrading to you.
- Speak with people in your community about the problem and what can be done.
- Report cases of child exploitation to the authorities concerned.
- Learn more about child labor and the laws against it.
- Ask your government to ratify and fully implement the Convention on the Worst Forms of Child Labor.
- Write letters to the editors calling for immediate action to end the worst forms of child labour.
- Tell businesses that you will buy nothing from them if they exploit children.
- Call your friends together and form a group united against the problem.
- Volunteer your time and support for organizations working to protect children.
- Pledge to continue your efforts until every child enjoys their right to a childhood.

As research on the Ghanaian rural child illustrates, a majority of them can neither read nor write. Given the lack of infrastructure and teachers in rural schools, low literacy rates exist among children who live and attend school in the rural regions. Statistics show that 60% of them do not acquire basic literacy (Berlan, 2004). This explains Berlan's concern about the guidelines above.

Another factor problematic with the above set of guidelines is the call on the children to ask the government of Ghana to ratify and to implement convention 182. In the first place, rural children do not know of any such convention, have no idea about the existence of the UN and its subsidiaries and ILO, and do not know of the Conventions that have been enforced to protect their rights and childhoods. It is for the same reasons that other activities by the Government of Ghana to secure the interests of its children have failed. According to the Director of WAJU, there exists the fear of not knowing where they would live and who would take care of them if they defy their parents or caretakers and report them to the police. Although this research did not evidence instances where domestic servants are made to accept domestic servitude under duress, my interviews with the Directors of WAJU and the Department of Social Welfare suggest that there are no official foster homes where abused children could stay when taken away from their parents. She states when asked if they had ever made an arrest about child labor exploitation

...You know may be the parent is the one who is trying to negotiate in such acts, and that child is still being cared for by that parent, so it is normally very difficult that we deal with such people, maybe send them to court to face the law, the rigors of the law or whatever it is. After these parents have been dealt with, who takes care of the child? There is no, there has never been any preparation, the government has never made, how do I say it, any convenient place to keep the people; we don't have proper places to keep such people. Sometimes when they are taken to even the children's home, we are told that they can never accept them. Some, of them they don't accept them, and even when they accept them, before they accept them you have to go to the social workers' or social welfare office to demand some documents, a whole lot of it before even the child can be admitted at the children's home. It is a very important thing that I have been asking the government or any agent to come out to help.

We observe from above that there are both national and international efforts to protect the Ghanaian child. Unfortunately, these efforts to protect them do not seem to be efficient, and many Ghanaian children continue to be overtly exploited through street work and petty trading. A major factor responsible for this is the disconnection between the realities that surround the vulnerability of children and the methods and processes of their protection. More importantly, these children are not aware of the existence of the many laws and institutions that exist to protect them.

CHAPTER SUMMARY AND CONCLUSION

Efforts to combat child labor exploitation and slavery culminate in the proliferation of international treaties to safeguard the interest and care of children. Internationally, any person below the age of 18 qualifies as a child. However, some scholars argue that this cutoff age impedes the campaign against child labor because it is merely a Western political construct which does not conform to the realities of some cultures. Childhood in many traditional cultures is defined by a person's dependence and lack of wealth. Many cultures require children to work not only to support their families but to be able to learn skills that would make them independent and productive members of society during adulthood. This, coupled with the flexibilities inherent in conventions such as C138 on Minimum Age, jeopardizes children's labor. Today, as pointed out, 250 million children work under exploitative conditions. It is estimated that 41%, i.e. about 80 million of all African children aged between 5 and 14 years, are victims of child labor exploitation (*African Business*, 1998; Innocenti Research Center, 2002). Chapter Five introduces the socio-cultural and economic environments within which children work in Ghana.

Chapter III

RESEARCH METHODS

As stated in Chapter One, this research employed both qualitative and quantitative methodologies to study child labor exploitation in domestic servitude in Ghana. The quantitative analyses applied a nationwide research that the Ghana Statistical Service conducted at the request of the Government, while the qualitative analyses derive from interviews that I conducted in three cities and four villages in Ghana. This chapter outlines the techniques of sample selection and explains the reasons behind the application of these methodologies and the research site.

QUALITATIVE RESEARCH METHODS

The data that I used for this part of the study were obtained from a qualitative research that I conducted in the summer of 2003. The main goal of the qualitative part of this study was to explore child domestic servitude in Ghana. I wanted to obtain firsthand descriptive information about the domestic servants, their experiences while in servitude, and the reasons for their enrollment into this type of activity. This exploratory approach was deemed appropriate because no documented systematic research focused specifically on Ghana's child domestic servants prior to this study. Their obscurity within the household setup also meant that they could not be subjected to any method of probabilistic sampling technique. Therefore, I had to begin the research through the qualitative approach.

MAP OF GHANA

Adapted from http://upload.wikimedia.org/wikipedia/commons/3/3e/Ghana_regions_named.png

GHANA
Incidence of Poverty - 1999

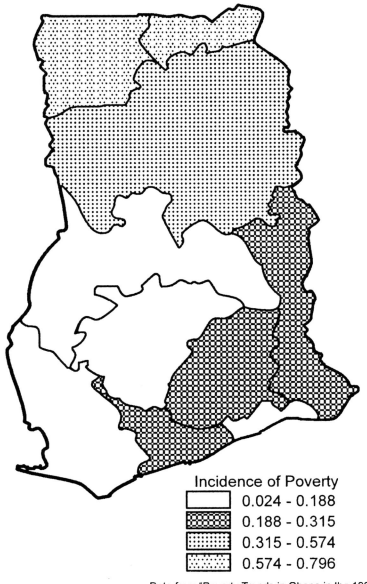

Incidence of Poverty

☐	0.024 - 0.188
▨	0.188 - 0.315
▦	0.315 - 0.574
░	0.574 - 0.796

Data from "Poverty Trends in Ghana in the 1990s'
Ghana Statistical Service - 2000

Research Sites

Interviews were conducted in four rural and three urban communities. The four rural communities are Hwidiem in the Ashanti Region, Nankasido, and Saltpond in the Central Region, and Tikobo #1 in the Western Region (refer to map on page 30). Although Tikobo #1 and Saltpond are rural communities, I operationalized them as semi-rural in this study because they have formal institutions such as banking, manufacturing firms, and good schools. The three cities were Accra, the capital of Ghana and the Greater Accra Region; Cape Coast, the capital of Central Region; and Kumasi, the capital of Ashanti Region.

A World Bank report estimates the population of Accra at 2.2 million (The World Bank, 2002). This accounts for about 25% of total urban population. As the capital of the country, Accra is home to Ghanaians from all ethnic backgrounds and to the head offices of major financial institutions, government institutions, parastatals, and multinational corporations. It is the destination of many rural migrants most of whom confine themselves to the shantytowns along the edges of the city (Ghana Home Page, 2004). Accra boasts of Ghana's premier university, the University of Ghana (at Legon), and many new private universities. The best hotels and entertainment facilities are also concentrated in this city. Accra and the neighboring Tema, located 20 miles east of the former, have the largest number of the industries, both micro enterprises and large plants, in Ghana (The World Bank, 2002).

Kumasi is the second largest city in Ghana and is located approximately 250 kilometers northwest of Accra. It accounts for about 15% of total urban population in Ghana (The World Bank, 2002). In 2000, a nationwide census estimated the population of Kumasi at about 1.7 million. Kumasi is the capital of Ashanti Region. Like Accra, it is the destination for many rural migrants from the poorer regions of Northern, Upper East and Upper West as well as from rural areas in the Ashanti Region. Kumasi is home to the University of Science and Technology, a polytechnic, as well as many vocational and training institutes and high schools.

Cape Coast, the third major town where I interviewed domestic servants, employers, and a non-formal recruiter, is the capital city of the Central Region. It is located along the Gulf Coast nearly 78 miles west of Accra. In terms of population, Cape Coast is not as large as the other two cities. A 2000 nationwide census estimates its population at 82,291. It is, however, considered the cradle of formal education in Ghana. It is home to the only university which for a long time specialized in research and the training of teachers, the University of Cape Coast where I received my baccalaureate degree. Most of the leading and elite high schools are located in this city. The leading role of Cape Coast in quality education derives from its status as the capital of the region where the first European missionaries and colonizers settled in the late 15th century. Among its major tourist attractions is the Cape Coast Castle where a large number of West African slaves were kept and later shipped to the Americas.

Hwidiem is a very small village in Ashanti Region, located approximately 25 miles north of Kumasi. The 2000 nationwide census sets its population at about 340. At the time of this research, Hwidiem was yet to be connected to the national electricity grid. It had no pipe-borne water, and women and children had to walk at least one mile to fetch either spring water or water from a stream. Unlike other towns where I collected data, this village had no marketplace. Some women took advantage of its location on the main trunk road that joins Kumasi and the district capital of Mampong to sell fruits, vegetables, and tubers to motorists. At the center of the village, I saw a small kiosk in which a woman sold convenience items. As will be illustrated in the Chapter on education, Hwidiem has only one primary school. Students and pupils have to travel to nearby villages to further their education.

In the Western Region, I interviewed recruiters, current and former domestic servants, and employers at Tikobo #1 and Bonyere. Bonyere is as poor as Hwidiem. The difference between the two villages lies in the fact that unlike Bonyere, Hwidiem is located on a major trunk road and thus is easily accessible. Tikobo # 1, a bigger town, can boast of a private clinic, a rural bank, and a Dutch owned coconut-fertilizer manufacturing factory. Tikobo #1 also has a private elementary school, with grades one through the junior secondary school, and a public school with the same grades.

Sampling Techniques in the Qualitative Method

Given the lack of reliable statistics and scholarly information on domestic servants, I could not employ any method of probabilistic sampling technique in this study. Additionally, I presumed that domestic servants would be afraid to talk to me, a stranger, while they were still in servitude. This fear, I thought, would be alleviated if I contacted them in the company of someone that they knew or if they were convinced an acquaintance or family member sent me to them. I further assumed that it would be impossible to be granted permission to interview a domestic if I went through their employers. In view of this, I considered the snowball sampling technique to be the most appropriate.

In addition, I selected the convenience sampling technique to supplement the snowball sampling. This was due to the fact that I believed domestic servants were easily identifiable by people who have encountered them before and from the fear that employers would not allow interviews with their servants. I anticipated that the supplementary use of convenience sampling technique would enhance access to domestic servants outside their homes for interview appointments. While this approach worked in terms of getting domestic servants to talk to without always having to go through the snowball technique, the reality was quite different; most of the employers permitted interviews with their domestic servants and some of them went a step further to grant me interviews themselves.

As someone who had lived with and encountered domestic servants among the research population, I considered myself a mere informed researcher whose status augmented the use of the two non-probabilistic sampling techniques mentioned above. In regard to the snowball technique, I knew *a priori* where and how to approach domestic servants in the early stage of the fieldwork. My application of the convenience sampling technique was also possible because I could identify domestic servants before they had been introduced to me as such.

I was aware of where to locate my respondents. One could see them in schools, in the streets, on the markets and in churches. What domestic servants did in these locations made it possible to differentiate them from non-domestic servants. I knew, for instance, that domestic servants took their employers' children to school in the mornings and went for them late in the afternoons. At the market place or at shopping centers, domestic servants either sell or buy foodstuffs for the households in which they live (Shoishab, 1997). On many occasions, they go in the company of their employers and carry the wares on their heads while they walk from stall to stall. At church, if the employing households have young children, the domestic servant takes care of them by changing and feeding them. She is usually dressed differently from the rest of the children in the family. She does not usually look cheerful especially if in the company of the employers themselves.

Given this background knowledge, I occasionally went to the schools when I knew that the domestic servants would be arriving so that I could interview them. The maidservants either carry the children on their back, if the latter were very young, or just walked them, at times, holding their hands. This approach of convenience sampling technique was not successful as employers were still home when domestic servants sent their children to school and were expecting them back within a specified period. Therefore, the girls turned down the request to be interviewed for fear that they would be late returning home and could be punished. Only one girl, about 10 years old, agreed to allow me to accompany her to seek permission from her madam. Having had employers who were so permissive of me and even volunteered to participate in this research, I accompanied this child, thinking that her employer was not going to be different from the others. Contrary to my expectations, she refused the interview.

In that particular incident, the girl was somewhat hesitant when I first approached her. However, when she understood the purpose of my interview, she agreed, but asked me to come home with her since her madam expected her back within a specific period. The walk to her house took about six minutes. The house was a two-storey roadside building that towered above the rest of the houses along the road. But for the dust which emanated from passing vehicles and covered mostly the base of this building, the house looked newly constructed and very prominent. A high wall bordered the building, making it difficult for pedestrians to see its inner features on the lower floor. My designated respondent rang a doorbell, and after about a minute her madam opened the door. We exchanged greetings and I explained my mission to her. She reluctantly permitted me into the building. Inside, were two vehicles, one an old Mercedes Benz. An American flag hung on the Mercedes, so I presumed either the entire family or the woman's husband had lived or was living in America. The domestic servant went inside to take the child off her back. She brought me a seat, and we started the interview. However, a minute into the interview, an unpleasant madam returned from the main building and asked that I stop the interview because they had a doctor's appointment. I apologized, thanked her, and asked if it was okay for me to come back at a more convenient time. She was not sure because she did not know when they were going to be home. I believed that she was never going to allow the interview and so did not return.

Ten of the respondents at Accra were selected through the approach of convenience sampling technique outlined above. Through the snowball approach, such respondents helped me to identify other domestic servants. Mansah, one of the domestic servants whom I identified through this approach, helped to find other servants with whom I could talk. When I met her, she carried a big container that seemed heavy because of the way she tilted towards one side. I asked her a few preliminary questions and confirmed that she was indeed a domestic servant. She had arrived at Accra less than a month earlier to work for an Accra-based petty trader whose name she did not even know. She was one of many girls who worked for this woman. Like other domestic servants, she expressed her fears about being seen with me. She was also afraid that if she stayed longer than it usually took her to run that particular errand, she would probably be punished.

I, therefore, made an appointment with her for the next morning. I did tell her about my intentions to interview her as well as the purpose of that interview. True to her word, she came back the next morning for our interview. She promised to help me interview other servants in that household, but said that I could not follow her to these other girls. On the second day, she came back to my house, in the company of a younger domestic servant, thirteen years old at the time of the interview. I nicknamed her Selasie. Selasie had been living with her employer for an estimated nine to eleven years. Although Mansah promised to bring more domestic servants, I never saw her again. I could not go to her address to look for her because of my promise to her that I would not get her into trouble with her employer.

Tikobo #1 is the other town where I had to use the convenience sampling technique. In this town, I went to the main shopping area, also the market place and got two shopkeepers who were domestic servants. Through them, I was able to talk to an employer, two recruiters, and four more domestic servants.

The Sample

I interviewed 86 respondents. Apart from two government officials who participated in this study, I assigned fictitious names to the other 84. Most of the 86 respondents were identified through the snowball sampling technique, while the rest were selected through the convenience sampling technique. I approached respondents at shops, near schools where I suspected they would be dropping off or picking up their employers' children, or simply knocked and entered homes in some of the elite neighborhoods to look for potential respondents. There were 44 current domestic servants, 14 former domestic servants, seven parents, six agents of recruitment, two government officials, and 13 employers.

The current domestic servants had either dropped out of school or had just graduated from the junior secondary school (J.S.S.). There were 16 current domestic servants who had dropped out of school, while 18 had completed the J.S.S. Three of them were still in school. Seven current domestic servants never went to school. The oldest person in this sample was a 28-year-old woman whom I met at one of the two employment agencies that I discuss shortly. She was also the only domestic servant respondent who had completed the senior secondary school (S.S.S.). The second oldest person was 25 years old and was recruited at the age of 15. She had dropped out of school. Three of my respondents were recruited around the age of six. However, at the time of this research, the youngest person was 8. There were four other participants who were as young as 12; the rest were between the ages of 13 and 20.

I interviewed 14 former domestic servants in various communities in Ashanti, Central, and Western Regions. I categorized them into older cohorts of domestic servants who lived in other households prior to Ghana's implementation of neo-liberal economic policies in the 1980s, and younger cohorts who were recruited afterwards. There were six former domestic servants who worked in other households before the 1980s and eight others who worked afterwards. At some point, all six of the respondents among the older generation were given the chance to go to school; only one of them remained there until the end of the primary school.

Esther, the only semi-educated among the six older cohorts of domestic servants, was also the only respondent in this category who could tell me her age and the exact year of her enrollment into domestic servitude. The rest found it difficult making references to exact timelines. They did not know their current ages or when they were enrolled into domestic servitude. Born in 1955, Esther agreed to live with a nurse who was looking for a babysitter while the latter migrated to the city to further her education. At the time, Esther was 11 years old. When I met her for this interview in 2003, she was a housewife. The others had become petty traders or fishmongers.

A majority of these participants belonged to the Akan ethnic groups, consisting of Ashanti from the Ashanti Region, Nzema/Ahanta from the Western Region, Fante from the Central Region, and Akuapim from the Eastern Region. With the exception of the Akuapim, all these Akan ethnic groups are matrilineal. Among the Akuapim, one observes both matrilineal and patrilineal systems of ancestry. People from all the northernmost regions of Ghana practice patrilineal systems. These include the Kusasi in the Upper East Region and the Dagomba in the Northern Region.

Semi-Structured Interviews

The qualitative interviews were semi-structured, which asked mostly open-ended questions. These questions related to the subjects' working conditions and experiences as domestic servants, the structures of the households from which they came, processes of recruitment, and the economy of their households. The questions also enquired about the domestic servants' level of autonomy and the factors that lead parents to send their children into domestic servitude.

As regards the servants' working conditions and experiences, I wanted to know how long domestic servants work per day, if they are abused and what forms such abuses took, and if they were paid and the forms such remunerations took. I asked almost all the respondents if any arrangements about the type and method of remuneration were made at the time of their enrollment into servitude. Prior to the fieldwork, I was aware that most of the domestic servants in Ghana were not paid at all. However, some of them were provided the means to learn a trade after staying with their employers for several years. Employers gave their domestic servants sewing machines and/or paid their starting fees for them to enroll in an apprenticeship in hairdressing or dressmaking. In the event that the child escaped because of inability to endure abuses and long hours of work, or if they were sent back to their parents for truancy or unsatisfactory performance, they might not gain anything at all. If they were paid in cash, I wanted to know who was the primary beneficiary of that income.

This research also investigated the level of autonomy that the child domestic servant exercised over her or his employment, the incomes or remunerations accruing to him or her, and her or his ability to exit servitude whenever she or he deemed it appropriate. The literature on child labor and child slavery points to scholars' identification of victim's level of autonomy as an important explanatory factor of new forms of slavery. In defining sexual slavery, for instance, Kathleen Barry (1984) highlights the significance of autonomy when she argued that slavery exists in "ALL situations where women or girls cannot change the immediate conditions of their existence; where regardless of how they got into those conditions they cannot get out; and where they are subject to sexual violence and exploitation" (Barry, 1984: 39-40). In a more recent publication, Kevin Bales (2000, 1999) identifies subjection of the victims to violent control and the loss of their freewill as the major defining factors of slavery. Given these views on contemporary slavery and prior research and interpretations of old forms of slavery, I was interested in finding out if these child domestic servants could exercise the level of autonomy that disqualified them as contemporary slaves.

Additionally, I wanted to know if the domestic servants that I interviewed in this research were slaves. More specifically, I wanted to know if they freely accepted or volunteered to work for their employers. For that reason, questions relating to the level of autonomy delved into the processes through which they were recruited, negotiations of their working conditions, processes of their exit from servitude, and how their incomes were disbursed. I was interested in finding out if participants could voluntarily leave the job without creating any problem between them and their parents or family members on one hand or between their families and their employers on the other.

This study further investigated the impact of gender roles and expectations on child domestic servitude. That women and girls spend more hours providing services in the private domestic sphere has long been established. I, however, asked parents whose children work or worked as domestic servants and the employers themselves if they had any sex preference in the recruitment of children into domestic servitude and what reasons they had for their preference. Additionally, I asked parents which of the sexes they were more likely to enroll into domestic servitude and why that was their choice.

Qualitative Data Analyses

Given the partial influence of interpretative sociology on this research, I collected data bearing in mind that the respondents, rather than I, are the experts in their lives and the meanings that they attach to their experiences as domestic servants. I adopted this approach to analyses from Anne Kasper's *A Feminist, Qualitative Methodology: A Study of Women with Breast Cancer* (1994). Kasper used the interpretative approach in that study and saw the respondents as the experts of their lives and the meanings that their lives had for them and their beliefs. She identified herself as an informed researcher and developed a three-part approach to data analyses. In the first part, Kasper sought to recognize and to capture the meanings and understandings that the respondents shared about their breast cancer crisis. In the second and third parts, Kasper's position as an informed researcher came into play. She looked for "the connections between facts and meanings presented in an individual's account..." to "...uncover how events and meanings..."were related to over-arching themes in each of her respondent's crisis (276) and to link individual accounts to the other respondents. In the third stage, she focused on the relationship between the general themes discovered in the previous stages to the study's theoretical framework.

Following that approach, I developed a three-stage methodology in the analyses of the qualitative data. I devoted the first stage of my analyses to the meanings that respondents have about their positions as past or current domestic servants, a parent of a domestic servant, or an employer. In the second stage, I connected events such as the death of a parent, the death of an employer or a parents' childhood experience, and the understandings that respondents shared about their lives. Given that my respondents were heterogeneous because they occupied different positions either as past or present domestic servants, paid or unpaid workers, parents or employers, I had to draw links within homogenous groups and at the next stage see how they related to the other groups. Within the same homogenous group, I compared individual accounts to the rest of their group members. In the last stage of the qualitative analyses, I located the generally observed patterns in the theoretical framework and formulated the hypothesis for the quantitative analyses.

QUANTITATIVE METHODS EMPLOYED IN THIS STUDY

Chapter Two of this book outlines some domestic and international efforts to eradicate child labor exploitation. Among them is ILO's International Program on the Elimination of Child Labor (IPEC), which is a guide to the organization's Convention on the Elimination of the Worst Forms of Child Labor (C182). IPEC primarily aims at the progressive elimination of child labor. Within the framework of this program, ILO endeavors to assist with the development and implementation of national policies on issues related to child labor, help create national awareness of problems associated with the incidence of child labor, and to promote the development and application of protective legislation in party states, among many other objectives some of which were mentioned in Chapter Two. Following these objectives of IPEC, the Ghana Statistical Service, in the early 1990s, conducted a pilot study on street children in the country. Based on the findings and the need for the country to build a databank on the incidence of child labor exploitation to facilitate efforts to eradicate this phenomenon, the government requested a more comprehensive research on child labor exploitation. Consequently in January 2001, the Ghana Statistical Services, in collaboration with the Ministry of Employment and Social Welfare, undertook more comprehensive household-based survey. As indicated earlier, I employed data from that research for the quantitative analyses in this project.

The quantitative analyses were carried out in three stages. The first stage examined univariate distribution of dependent and independent variables for the child workers in this study. Both dependent and independent variables were mostly categorical. Therefore, the second stage of the analyses tested the existence of bivariate associations among relevant variables, using chi square statistics. In the third stage, logistics regression analyses were performed on dummy dependent variables. Some of the dependent variables for the logistics regression analyses were obtained from transformation of variables that had more than two categories. The following subsections outline the univariate analyses.

Univariate Distribution of Dependent and Independent Variables

The findings of the qualitative analyses informed variable selection for the quantitative analyses. I observed from the interviews that lineage, education, sex, and respondents' origins are some of the variables that influence child domestic servitude in Ghana. Unfortunately, not all patterns of dependent and independent variable relationships that the qualitative analyses evidenced could be subjected to statistical analyses given the nature of the statistical data that this research employed.

There were 17,034 respondents made up of 8,871 (52%) males and 8,163 (48%) females aged between five and 17 years old. The average age was 10.6 with a modal and median age of 10 years respectively. The standard deviation of the mean was 3.58. Table 3.1 provides the age distribution in detail.

Table 3.2 presents of the regional distribution of all respondents in the survey. The largest proportion of respondents, 2,623 (constituting 15.4% of the sample) came from the Ashanti Region. The next largest proportion of 14% came from the Northern Region. Respondents from the two smallest regions of Upper East and Upper West provided 1,027 (6%) and 773 (4.5) respectively. The rest of the regional distribution of the sample is presented in the Table.

OPERATIONALIZING CHILD DOMESTIC SERVITUDE

The data obtained from Ghana Statistical Service does not define the variable of child domestic servants or servitude. Therefore, using the variables of "relationship to the head of household" and "employment status," this research operationalized child domestic servants to consist of all unpaid family workers or domestic servants below the age of 18, who are not the heads of their households, and who do not live with their parents, spouses, in-laws, or siblings. In other words, "child domestic servants" in the quantitative part of this study refers to those who describe their employers or household heads as non-relatives or other relatives. This definition derives from my observation from the qualitative interviews that domestic servants combine trading and household responsibilities and at times define their employers as relatives but could not specify the nature of the relationship.

Table 3.1: Age Distribution of the Sample

	Frequency	Percentage
5	1,291	7.6
6	1,485	8.7
7	1,536	9.0
8	1,451	8.5
9	1,357	8.0
10	1,598	9.4
11	1,150	6.8
12	1,546	9.1
13	1,246	7.3
14	1,197	7.0
15	1,370	8.0
16	994	5.8
17	813	4.8
Total	**17,034**	**100.0**

Table 3.3 provides frequency distribution of respondents' relationships to their household heads. Response categories to this variable are "head," "spouse," "child," "brother/sister," "grandchild," "son/daughter-in-law," "other relatives," and "non-relatives." We observe in that table that a large number of respondents are the children of the household heads. While such children may be engaged in some type of economic activities, what distinguished them from other child workers is that they enjoy the love and support they could easily access by living with their families.

Table 3.2: Regional Distribution of the Sample

	Frequency	Percentage
Western	1,724	10.1
Central	1,396	8.2
Greater Accra	2,009	11.8
Volta	1,372	8.1
Eastern	1,951	11.5
Ashanti	2,623	15.4
Brong Ahafo	1,765	10.4
Northern	2,394	14.1
Upper East	1,027	6.0
Upper West	773	4.5
Total	**17,034**	**100.0**

Table 3.3: Respondents' Relationship to their Heads of Household

	Frequency	Percentage
Head	3	.0
Spouse (husband/wife)	15	.1
Child	13,161	77.3
Brother/sister	233	1.4
Grandchild	2,083	12.2
Son/daughter -in-law	32	.2
Other relative	1,258	7.4
Non-relative	249	1.5
Total	**17,034**	**100.0**

Table 3.4: Distribution of Child Workers

	Frequency	Percentage
Grandchild/Child	15,244	91.0
Other relatives	1,258	7.5
Non-relatives	249	1.5
Total	**16,751**	**100.0**

Tables 3.4 and Table 3.5 show two new variables I recoded from the variable of "relationship to the head of household." The first is the new variable of "child workers" which excluded household heads, spouses, brothers/sisters, and son/daughter-in-laws, but includes children/grandchildren of household heads, other relatives and non-relatives. Table 3.4, which is a distribution of the new variable of "child workers," indicates that 91% of all children in the survey are grandchildren or children of the head of the household. Table 3.5 is a repetition of Table 3.4 but excludes the first response category of grandchild/child. We notice that 1507 respondents are the domestic servants. They are children who live with people they define as other relatives or non-relatives and are engaged in various types of unpaid work, prominent among them being the provision of domestic services.

Table 3.5: Distribution of Child Servants

	Frequency	Percentage
Other relatives	1,258	83.5
Non-relatives	249	16.5
Total	**1,507**	**100.0**

Table 3.6: Employment Status of the Sample

	Frequency	Percentage
Employer	3	0
Employee (full-time)	26	.54
Employee (part-time)	25	.50
Casual employee	70	1.5
Own account worker	414	8.6
Unpaid family worker	4,098	85.6
Domestic Employee	38	.8
Paid apprentice	10	.1
Unpaid apprentice	104	2.2
Total	**4,788**	**100.0**

CHAPTER SUMMARY AND CONCLUSION

The methodologies that I employed in this study were primarily qualitative and exploratory. The lack of existing research on child domestic servitude in general and Ghana's domestic servants in particular made me choose these methods. Given that surveys in previous research on child labor did not successfully explore child domestic servitude, I used the snowball and convenience sampling techniques in order to gain access to the domestic servants. These approaches required that I begin the interviews in areas where I was sure I could get domestic servants to participate in the research without their fearing punishment from their employers.

Chapter IV

PROCESSES OF RECRUITMENT AND THE NATURE OF RELATIONSHIPS BETWEEN DOMESTIC SERVANTS AND THEIR EMPLOYERS

In this and the following chapters, I discuss the interviews that I had with the various sets of samples. This chapter focuses on the processes of recruitment and the role of families in the recruitment of their members into servitude. Given that urban regions tend to be more attractive, parents either look for urban households for their children to live in with, or accept offers presented to them by recruiters. Children who complete basic education and do not have any hopes of continuing their education or learning a trade if they remain in their households also look for and or accept offers of domestic servitude. In this research, I discovered three vital approaches through which children are recruited into domestic servitude. I refer to them as formal, non-formal, and informal processes of recruitment respectively. I discuss these three approaches of recruitment in the following subsections. I begin with a discussion of the structures and role of both rural and urban families in the recruitment of children into domestic servitude.

RURAL VERSUS URBAN FAMILY STRUCTURES AND THEIR INFLUENCE ON THE RECRUITMENT OF CHILDREN INTO DOMESTIC SERVITUDE

Domestic servants are usually recruited from rural regions for urban households. Rural families typically live in overcrowded buildings that house numerous households. Often, these are extended families in which grand and great-grandmothers, uncles, and aunts as well as cousins pool and share resources. The crowding pertaining to rural areas in Ghana is also present in urban communities. There are compound houses that are occupied by households which in some cases are made up of families that are not related in any way. These are poor families who do not have domestic servants. Where such households live with domestic servants, the latter are recruited primarily for petty trading purposes. Mansah, Selasie and Serena (whom I introduced in Chapter Three), lived with such families at Accra. The first two families that Samira lived with also shared these attributes.

Conversely, employing households are almost always economically comfortable, with at least one of the parents earning a fixed salary or occupying a high ranking position in a government or private organization. In this research, there were university professors, high school teachers, government officials, and self employed businessmen and women who hired domestic servants. There was one air hostess and one Member of Parliament.

Unlike their counterparts in rural households or among the urban poor, employing households have between one and four children. This makes it easier for them to reduce overcrowding in rooms and to be able to ensure that their children receive the highest level of education that they would want to attain. In about six households, I found out that the employers' children lived in either Europe or North America. There were other adult children of employers who lived in other parts of the country. If young children were not home at the time of this research, they were usually living in boarding houses as students.

In some cases, children whose parents are otherwise well off end up in domestic servitude upon the death of their parents and in the absence of an honest successor to take care of the orphans. Although it is rare for urban poor to find themselves in domestic servitude, instances of extended family members succeeding and usurping the properties of the deceased drive some urban children to live in servitude. In this research, I interviewed three domestic servants who ended up in domestic servitude under similar circumstances; two of them were sisters who lived part of their childhood as domestic servants because their uncle, who inherited their deceased father's timber factory, failed to take care of them. Although their mother did not live in a village, she could not afford to take care of all four children.

Although a majority of my respondents moved from rural areas to urban centers, a number of them had moved from rural-to-rural, rural to semi-urban, or from semi-urban to semi-urban areas. The processes of recruitment which my respondents reported did not differ much between rural-semi-urban and rural-urban employments. Limited observations indicate that the rural-rural recruitment was markedly different from the other two types. I interviewed only one former domestic servant who lived with her father's friend in a rural community so that she could attend school in a nearby village. During my visit to this village, I observed that a number of households lived with distant relatives and at times with people that they were not related to in any way. However, children who find themselves in such situations are given the opportunity to attend school and to enjoy their childhood—at least within the rural context—this being significantly different from the out-group positions that domestic servants in urban areas endured.

Interviews with parents and unobtrusive questions included in my interviews with the children pointed to the influence of parental occupation on children's vulnerability to labor exploitation and slavery. Some cultures require both boys and girls to enter the labor market as part of their socialization processes. In the population of study, the type of training that a child receives during socialization tends to be culturally and geographically specific. Different geographic areas in Ghana specialize in different economic activities; this has historically determined what children learn through informal socialization. Among rural Ashantis and the populations of other forest areas in Ghana, boys and girls learn gender-related farming skills before they become adults. Girls are made to learn how to use the hoe to clear weeds from farms and to gather forage or uproot tubers while boys focus on clearing the land for farming. Back home, both boys and girls fetch water from the streams and rivers. The girl's day will not end there; she will continue running errands to assist her mother in preparation of the evening meal and to clean afterward, while the boys spend time interacting with male adults of their households.

I observed that the amount of control that children have over themselves was important in their recruitment. In both rural and urban households, children have limited autonomy over their lives. Following Western legal traditions that I discussed earlier, children in former colonies in Sub-Saharan Africa cannot sign contracts, open bank accounts, access courts, or accept job offers (Ramanathan, 2000; Landsdown, 1994). Traditional expectations of children in the research population take these attributes of minors to a different level. In Ghana, children are less powerful relative to adult members of their households. Both traditional patterns of socialization and formal educational texts socialize Ghanaian children to acknowledge and internalize the superiority of adults by respecting and obeying them (Berlan, 2004). The popular adage that children must be seen rather than heard makes it less likely for them to question decisions made on their behalf by other members of their households. Parents and adults in general have utmost authority over children. This gives adults in the child's immediate, as well as their extended families, the decision-making power over them. As I observed with the recruitment of Akosua, one of the respondents in this research, both extended and nuclear family members came together to negotiate with the university professor who recruited her.

Current and former domestic servants indicated that their parents were the decision makers as far as their statuses as domestic servants were concerned. The only difference I observed in this regard is the fact that a majority of contemporary domestic servants were old enough to decide with their parents regarding their employment into domestic servitude, while the older generation of servants were relatively younger and had no say whatsoever when their parents sent them away. Five of the six older cohorts of domestic servants said their parents made decisions about their recruitment and work for other families. Only one former domestic servant from the pre-1980 era, Esther, was different from the other, older participants. Esther voluntarily and willingly decided to look for somebody to live with when she had a misunderstanding with her maternal grandmother. She lived with more than one family and, unlike the other respondents in her generation, received partial pay for her services in some cases while one family promised her the usual sewing machine.

Responses by the other domestic servants as regards the role of their parents included "they gave birth to me so I had to come," "I had finished school and wasn't doing anything so I wanted to come," I was always wishing that I could get somewhere to go since I was basically idle," and "I didn't like going to the farms so much so it was a great opportunity for me to leave the village." With the exception of the first response, the above illustrate a relatively lower dependence on parental expectations among contemporary domestic servants who participated in this research. My observation is that for such domestic servants, while parents were willing to put their feet down towards their enrollment into domestic servitude, the position of the child was significantly relevant, although not the most important determining factor.

All but seven of my domestic servant samples agreed that their parents or guardians had the final say in their work as domestic servants. They stated further that it was a sign of respect to obey their parents under such conditions. In one particular case, a parent demonstrated his authority over his domestic-servant daughter by emphasizing that if the daughter, Esi, (who had been sending messages to her parents about the abuses she was experiencing) returned home today, he was going to send her back the next day. He asserted in his conversation with me that as the father, he had absolute control over his child and whatever he said would be final.

Samira's experience is typical in this case. When she left her step-grandmother because of maltreatment, she could have stayed with her own mother or grandmother and remained in school. However, her younger sister who was living with her mother's aunt, had run away to her father's village, also because of abuses.

Samira was given to this grandaunt in place of her younger sister so that the relationship between her mother and her extended family members would not be mired. Her mother insisted that Samira lived with this relative against the latter's will.

PROCESSES OF RECRUITMENT

This research discovered three patterns of recruitment of domestic servants. In none of these three processes of recruitment did I observe the use of force to recruit the servants, although underage children are not adequately knowledgeable and mature enough to consent to their enrollment. In the following subsections, I discuss the three types of recruiters I found under each pattern. There is a significant difference between the processes of recruitment for girls who were employed between 1980 and 2003 and those who were recruited in the years before. Cultural practices and beliefs influenced the recruitment of older domestic servants; therefore, both close and distant family members were those who arranged to either live with younger relatives or to send them to other relatives.

Formal Recruiters

formal recruiters are registered employment agencies that specialize in the recruitment of domestic workers, house-boys, garden-boys, and cooks. Formal employment agencies have not always existed in Ghana; they are a recent development. The first such organization was established in the early 1970s. My informant, a chief and brother of the founder of this organization, could not give the exact date of establishment because it became defunct on the death of the founder, his sister. This foundation concentrated on the recruitment, training, and assignment of domestic servants who were old enough to work. The late sister, a Canadian-trained nurse, decided to found this organization in order to help curb the abuses and exploitation that young women and girls had to endure in domestic servitude. I learned while collecting the data that there were five such organizations, but I was able to locate two of them for interviews.

Domestic Services Agency at Dansoman. While introducing myself to a domestic servant's employer for the permission to allow the interview, she launched into her own complaints which eventually made her a respondent. It was in the course of this interview that I learned about the first formal agency. I made a call to the director and got an appointment for the next day. This was a home-based office, located on a very busy road connecting Dansoman, a somewhat affluent suburb of Accra. Behind his small office in the same house lies a stretch of lawn in the middle of which stood an avocado pear tree. It was under this tree that we conducted the more-than-one-hour-long interview.

His only employee in this organization was an office assistant. Prospective domestic servants had to submit an application plus a fee, which at the time of this study was C15,000.00 (approximately $2.00). The agency further required a police report on applicants, and for that, prospective domestic servants had to pay an additional fee of C30,000.00. Besides personal information and contacts, applicants need to provide two guarantors who can be police officers, clergymen, military personnel, or civil servants. The average age of applicants is 21 and the minimum age 18. Usually, prospective employees simply walked in looking for jobs. When this agency ran short of applicants, they sent word through their recruits to contact relatives or friends who could be looking for jobs.

Clients seeking domestic servants must register with the agency. They pay a C65,000 "retainer fee" which, according to the director, goes towards the background search of prospective servants. How much domestic servants earn depends on what the employer is willing to pay. Employers also pay an equivalent of a month's salary to the agency. In 2003, monthly salaries ranged between C100,000 and C200,000, which is about US$15-30. Clients who offer the lowest pay of C100,000 per month agree to provide toiletries, food, and clothing until the end of the employees' service. When approved, employees who go through the agency have to sign a contract. If they violate contractual conditions, they forfeited a month's salary.

Domestic servants may encounter problems ranging from culture shock through communication problems. According to the director, recruits complained of not being able to go to bed early and to have off days. They also did not like their inability to walk in and out of their homes as they pleased and of communication problems. In regard to the communication problem, this director believed that it existed where both client and domestic servants spoke different languages and so had to use English as the means of communication. Given the low literacy rates among them, domestic servants were not fluent in the English language.

Domestic Services Agency at Tesano. One morning while driving through the streets of Tesano, a major affluent community at Accra, I came across a billboard for this agency. When I visited the agency, I was able to talk to the director and two applicants. There were at least ten applicants who waited on pews to submit new applications, receive training, or to follow up on previous applications. Among them was a male who appeared to be in his late 30s to early 40s. He told me he came to apply for a job as a houseboy or a gardener. Almost all the females there appeared to be in their 20s or were older than that. There was an 18-year-old woman, a school drop out, who had migrated from the northern part of the country in search of a job. She lived with her brother's family but did not get along with his wife and so was looking for another place to stay. She hoped she would find live-in employment where she could stay.

The second respondent from this agency is the 28-year-old woman earlier mentioned. She lost both parents and could no longer fund her education and thus decided to look for a job. She heard about this organization through a friend. If given employment, this would be her third job through them. She lived with the first employer for about a year and received C300,000 until this employer returned to her home country, Nigeria. She got her second job through this agency, but the employer was not as generous as the former. She said that this employer, although a Nigerian too, had cultivated the "Ghanaian employer's habit of being mean." The employer had promised to pay her C200,000, but started her at C100,000 and refused to increase it. In addition, she did not permit this respondent and other household employees in her house to eat or make personal use of the resources available. As a result, she terminated her contract to look for another employer.

The process of recruitment was the same for this agency as the one at Dansoman. Applicants had to pay a registration fee and another fee for a background check. Prospective employers also bore a percentage of the fee for background check.

As following discussion illustrates, the processes of recruitment under these two formal agencies of employment differed markedly from non-formal and informal agents of recruitment. Their concern about the age of recruits and households in which these recruits would work created a safe environment for both employer and employee. Formal agencies protected their clients by ensuring that their recruits did not have any criminal backgrounds. The training for new recruits prepared them for their prospective households and provided them with the tools that would help them work satisfactorily while preparing them against physical and sexual abuses. Another important detail that was non-existent among the non-formal and informal recruitment processes was the negotiations that formal agencies held with clients on behalf of their recruits to ensure the latter received regular remuneration commensurate with the services provided.

Informal Recruiters

More often than not, urban residents who visit rural regions of the research population are met with repeated requests from parents to take one or two rural children with them to the cities. Even before I entered college, there were two children, a boy and a girl, whom I had been approached to take in to live with the moment I got out of school and became independent. While I was in college, residents in the villages where I collected data for my undergraduate research and worked as a research assistant requested that I come for their children and let them live with me when I graduated. In one such instance, a local interviewer I supervised told me his daughter was ready to move and live with me on campus if only I would say yes to their request. More recently, when I went to Ghana for this research, there were two more proposals; both requests came from two women in one of the villages I visited.

One of them was a middle-aged-looking woman, probably in her 30s, who asked me to help her migrate to the United States. She was prepared to do anything that I asked her, even to become a prostitute in exchange. When I returned to the same village a week later, to interview parents of former domestic servants, a respondent made a passionate plea to me to let her send at least one of her daughters with me. She did not care if I pushed them into prostitution.

Such approaches by parents and prospective domestic servants constitute the first type of informal recruitment. For the participants in this research, the informal process of recruitment tends to dominate, with appointments through family members being the most frequent.

Informal recruiters are the extreme opposites of formal recruiting agencies. They are the occasional intermediaries between prospective domestic servants and their employers and are neither registered nor regular recruiters. I identified three different types of informal recruiting. The first type involves family members who assist relatives either to recruit or to become domestic servants. The second type involves non-family members, while the third is a combination of both family and non-family members. In the first category parents are eager to let their children—both school going and non-school going—migrate to the cities to benefit from the many amenities that the city offers. The experiences that I shared in the previous paragraph typify the ways in which families try to look for employers for their children. Parents approach close and distant relatives, as well as non-relatives, when they cannot finance their children's education or when they want them to migrate to the cities.

For example, Esi, the last of six children, finished the J.S.S. at age 15 when her father retired. The parents were no longer on any substantial source of income and so could not fund her through the senior secondary school (S.S.S.). Given this background, her mother approached this respondent's employer requesting that Esi live with them and provide free domestic services for which she would be given a sewing machine and the apprenticeship fee at the end of two years. Such instances were commonplace in this study. What was unique about Esi's situation was the fact that when her mother was a child, she too lived with the employer's mother. Throughout my interview with Esi's parents, her mother referred to Esi's employer as her own sister and so would not pay any mind to complaints that the daughter had sent to them prior to my appearance. As tradition demands, Esi's father acknowledged his wife's professed relationship to her childhood employer's daughter by referring to the latter as his "wife" too.

Circumstances surrounding Serwah's recruitment depicts another approach through which family members participate in the recruitment processes of domestic servants. She came from the same village as her employer. This employer's aunt, a teacher in that village, served as recruiter for her nieces in the cities. This teacher approached Serwah one afternoon and asked if she was still in school. She had dropped out and was actually looking for a place to move to when the teacher spoke with her. She showed interest in going to live with the teacher's niece, a secondary school teacher, and from there, this recruiter went to see Serwah's mother who also agreed.

An example of non-family member recruitment was Angela's. This current domestic servant had lost both parents by age 12. Her uncle looked for someone for her to live with, but she had to quit after nine months for wrongful accusations, abuses, and threats to send her back without pay. She returned to her grandmother in the village. There, a former domestic servant who had had to return home for getting pregnant while a domestic servant recruited her. This recruiter pleaded with Angela's "father" (who was in actuality the uncle who succeeded her deceased father) and her grandmother to permit her employment because "... she didn't want..." Angela ... "to mess up" her "... life, get pregnant and loiter about aimlessly...," Angela explained. I asked Angela how her life was going to be better than her recruiter's since the latter got pregnant while in servitude, and she stated, "You should realize that if I live with my "father" and my grandmother, I won't be obedient to them. But when you live with different people, you have to listen to what they say before you can live with them." Angela said that she did not want to accept the offer initially because of her previous experience. However, she decided to do it after her uncle's persuasion.

The third type of informal recruitment is depicted in Akosua's employment where her family members and a non-relative initiated her recruitment. Akosua's uncle became the main intermediary between her family and her employer, although the whole recruitment process originated from a current domestic servant who came from her hometown and was working in Cape Coast where Akosua was to go. The elders of her extended family held discussions prior to the arrival of her employers, a university professor and his wife, a university staff member. In attendance were her mother, maternal grandmother, her mother's uncles and brothers. Her father was deceased at the time of her recruitment. She could not attend that meeting because "they are the elders," she said. She was close to 18 when she was employed and could have participated in the negotiations. However, given that many Ghanaian households adhere to the notion that the "child should only be seen and not heard" and the authority adult family members have over their children, she left the negotiations to her older family members.

Akosua's uncle disclosed proceedings at the meeting to her:

> When they came, the family asked what type of work I would be doing. And they said I would be doing housework, and no other work. We were told they would pay me 80 [C80,000], and my uncles said it wasn't enough. They [the employers] said I was going to be their responsibility, if I fell ill, it was their responsibility, my cream was their responsibility, my soap was their responsibility, my meals were their responsibility, everything was their responsibility, but if I were to do my hair, then that would be my only responsibility. But I wanted to do [relax] my hair but my mother and the others said they won't let me do it.

Such was the strength of this extended family's influence on Akosua that when asked if she was able to do her hair, she stated

> ...They asked me to go and cut it so I went in the company of a certain sister to cut it. When I finished..., when we were going, my mother told us that we shouldn't cut it too short. But they made it so short so when she saw it, she was like why did you sit down for them to cut it so short? I asked her not to bother me since she was the one who asked me to go and cut it.

All in all, these processes depict the families' and friends' eagerness to assist their young relatives and friends to migrate to the cities and towns to escape the harshness of village lives and to take advantage of the many amenities available in the cities. As Michel Bonnet notes,

> In an environment marked by large numbers of young people out of work and an education system offering members of the poorest parts of society, particularly in the Third World, virtually no chance at all of finding work, hunger pangs go hand in hand with the fear that children are about to fall victim to the worst of all possible ills ... Parents are tormented by worries for their children's future. All they want is to give their children the very best of what they have to offer—and what invaluable experience they have of the struggle to survive!—to equip them for life and, in short, help them develop, they hope, towards the longest possible future (Bonnet: 2000: 182-183).

This observation corroborates earlier research finding in other countries that parents did not only want their children to migrate to the cities for absolute poverty, but for relative poverty as well (Ramanathan, 2000). While absolute poverty refers to the lack of vital resources such as food, health, and shelter, relative poverty is concerned with taken-for-granted resources such as access to luxuries and, in this particular context, to the amenities in the cities.

Non-Formal Recruiters

Although different from the two other sources of recruitment, non-formal agents exhibit traits of both formal and informal recruiters. They are regular recruiters who, although not formally established as agents of employment, bring children from rural areas to other places to live with and work for other families. Like the informal processes of recruitment they too employ children of all ages, making these domestic servants most vulnerable to various forms of abuses and exploitation. I was able to interview four non-formal recruiters who had employed some of my respondents. I interviewed the first (nicknamed Derrick) at Accra. I met the second (nicknamed Sophia), a housewife who petty-traded in foodstuffs at Cape Coast.

I met the third non-formal recruiter (nicknamed Ali) in a semi-urban area at Tikobo #1 in the Western Region. An employer directed me to his shop where he sold canned foods and other convenience products. From Tikobo # 1, I went to a nearby village, Bonyere, where I interviewed the fourth non-formal recruiter (nicknamed Ahmed). In the following subsections, I give detailed accounts of my interviews with these non-formal recruiters.

Derrick: The Non-Formal Recruiter at Accra. I met three of Derrick's recruits but could interview only two of them. They were two girls and a boy. I interviewed the boy and one of the girls. All three of them had finished the junior secondary school (J.S.S.). The male lived with the female I could not interview in the same household. In that household was another male servant whose relative was the household head. It was during my interview with the male respondent that I learnt about this agent and took the directions to his house. A combination of the very poor and somewhat rich lived in that part of Accra.

Some time in 1985, Derrick's employer and owner of his current house, a university professor whose wife was a medical doctor, asked him to find a domestic servant from his hometown for them. This family had an only child and needed someone who would help around the house and keep their daughter company. Following that recruitment, the professor's friends and acquaintances always approached him to look for a helper or garden boy for them, with requests for female helpers being dominant. Derrick emphasized that his recruits work for university faculty and staff only, although the three I encountered worked for businessmen. I also learned from his interview that at least one of them lived with a high school administrator. According to him in 2003, when I conducted this research, he had recruited between 45 and 50 domestic servants and houseboys since 1985.

Most of his recruits were aged between 15 and 20, he told me. He usually brought them from his hometown in the Central Region or his wife's hometown in the Eastern Region. Two of the recruits came from his hometown, while the other was his wife's sister. Usually, Derrick's recruits completed the junior secondary school before he employed them and so were at least 15 years old. He told me that

> The people I bring them to ... are [university] lecturers who always speak
> English. The person who dropped out of school will have problems with the lan-
> guage, the language could be a problem but those who finished the J.S.S. could
> express themselves.

Contrary to this assertion, although the three recruits that I met had finished the J.S.S., they could not speak English. This was characteristic of most children who lived and went to school in rural Ghana.

Derrick looked for recruits for his elite clients. Nevertheless, parents did approach him whenever he visited his hometown, asking him to look for jobs or people for their children to live with in the cities. Michael is the male recruit that I interviewed. He had finished the J.S.S. and was neither going to school nor working when Derrick visited his hometown. Michael's mother was friends with Derrick's sister and on this occasion, the mother pleaded with him to find a job for her son. Michael explained that

> in response, Derrick said he didn't have any job for me. However, he was going to look for someone for me to live with so that I would be paid at the end of the month. He said I would save that income and when I got enough to go and learn a trade, I would ask permission to leave.

In explaining to me why they were willing to migrate with him to the cities, Derrick stated that in their

> Village, for instance, we see vehicles like once a week. I know some girls that I brought here some time ago and if you saw them, you might not believe she [they] had even lived in a village. The way they talked, dressed and their mannerisms had all changed. So they prefer to come to the cities to get polished or to learn.

He further stated that

> Pregnancy rates are higher in the rural area than here [Accra]. In all the ten years or fifteen years that I have been bringing children here, none of them has become pregnant. Most of the time, they live in a walled house and even where there is no security, you can't go out without being noticed. In the villages, however, the girls could just say they are visiting their friends and would be back soon, but might be going to see their men. So it is helpful when they come to the cities. There is another girl that I brought here eight years ago. All her peers have become pregnant or have given birth, but she is here and hasn't become pregnant. Her mother is therefore happy I got her out of the village.

Kate, one of the two females recruited by Derrick, was also his sister-in-law. At the time of this research, Kate had curtailed her "contract" with her first employer and had come to Derrick to be reassigned to another family. Kate's previous recruitment did not follow that pattern of parents approaching him for assistance with their children. She had finished the J.S.S. and was not working in her hometown when Derrick visited and asked "if I would like to go and live in Accra. I said yes, but asked him what I will be doing there? His response was that he would know what to do with me when we got there. His wife is my sister. He told my mother before bringing me," Kate explained. She stayed for one year and decided to leave because her employer's aunt who also lived in that house, maltreated her. At the time of her recruitment, Derrick arranged that the employer pay her off with a sewing machine, a trunk, or a suitcase filled with pieces of cloth at the end of two years. Given her early curtailment of this arrangement, she received only C300,000, i.e. a little less than US$40.00, for the entire year that she lived with and served that family. Derrick kept it for her while she waited to be reassigned.

Kate was not the only person among Derrick's recruits to have prematurely ended a "contract." Domestic helpers encounter a number of problems that drive them to quit, some without informing their employers. I learned through an employer that her husband sexually harassed some of the girls that Derrick brought to them. On a number of occasions they ran away. However, Derrick kept sending female recruits into this particular house. A couple of months after returning from Ghana, I found out that the other servant whom I could not interview had run away. She had made complaints about her employer's sexual harassment. Soon afterwards, Michael, the only male among Derrick's recruits who lived with this other girl, also escaped because his employer thought he had encouraged and assisted the female servant to escape. Prior to my departure, I spoke to Derrick about these allegations of sexual harassments. He denied the allegations associated with this particular household but discussed another instance where a servant made similar complaints and how he removed the girl from that household.

Like the other intermediaries in this research, Derrick acted as a surrogate parent for his recruits. He cited instances where his girls or boys living in neighboring households usually passed by to say hello when they went out to run errands. He told me that he also visited them from time to time to see how they were doing. Keeping Kate's send-off package was one of the roles he performed in his capacity as a surrogate parent.

When asked if he received pay for his services, he responded in the negative. He only received compensation or refunds when he used his own money to go for recruits. As to whether parents got paid when their children were taken away from them, he pointed out that

> The parents at times expect that after a year, they should be given part of their children's money. Some of the employers that the children live with do understand when I explain it to them, that it is they who gave birth to the children and so could give may be 200,000 to be given to the parents. There are those who argue that they [the parents] were supposed to take care of their children. They failed to do that and I am taking care of them so I have nothing to give them. So there are two things. There are those who understand, and those who will never understand.

Kate stated in her interview that Derrick once took money from her former employer for her mother. Derrick did not make the request for her mother to be paid. "Bro. Derrick said my mother extended her regards to me. She [employer] asked if he went to my mother and he said yes. Then she said that when he was leaving she would give him something to be given to my mother," Kate said.

Sophia: The Non-Formal Recruiter at Cape Coast. I met this recruiter, Sophia, through a domestic servant at Cape Coast. As stated earlier, she was a housewife whose husband occupied a mid-level managerial position at the university. She was in her sixth year of recruiting. Like Derrick, Sophia started recruiting children when a neighbor requested a child from her. Her recruits came from her hometown. They were usually between the ages of 12 and 17. I believed her recruits could be even younger because she considered those of age 14 to be old. When I met Sophia, she did not decline the interview, yet she was reluctant to provide information regarding her position as a non-formal recruiter, claiming that she had employed only one domestic servant for a family at Cape Coast. As the interview progressed, she contradicted herself by making references to other domestic servants whom she had recruited. Like other non-formal recruiters, Sophia was afraid I could be a government agent investigating the exploitation of children's labor.

Her recruits had not always completed the J.S.S.; some were school dropouts. Sophia usually arranged with employers to either pay her recruits regularly every month or to give them the accumulated wages at the end of an agreed period. Although she would not tell me how many girls she had brought to live with other families, I sensed that she had a very high rate of turnover. The longest staying domestic servant spent about a year. Two sisters whom she recruited for two different families received C80,000 and C50,000 respectively per month. Sophia kept the money for them. The sister who received C50,000 had to leave for misunderstandings with the employer. Her employer was dissatisfied with her and complained to Sophia. Around the same time, that particular recruit went to Sophia to express her displeasure with her employer and subsequently was assigned another household. I never had the opportunity to talk to her. However, Sophia said that recruit received a total of C450,000 for living in that household for nine months. The servant took C150,000 for personal effects and gave the rest to Sophia to save for her. Sophia never got remunerated for recruiting duties but at times received reimbursement for transportation from the employers.

Ali: The Non-Formal Recruiter at Tikobo #1. Ali and Ahmed are the other two recruiters whom I spoke to. They both came from the northern part of the country. These two recruiters shared a unique attribute that Sophia and Derrick did not have. Ali and Ahmed were former recruits themselves. Based on their community's perception of them, they became role models and, consequently, recruiters. Ali migrated to the south through a non-formal recruiter, who was also a northerner. He could not recall the exact year he was recruited; however, he had lived in the southern part of Ghana for over 20 years. Before 2003, he bought coffee from neighboring villages. He did not indicate where he sold it, but I assumed it was in the Côte d'Ivoire. Ali recalled the circumstances leading to his own migration to the south to justify his current "pastime" as a recruiter:

> Life was very difficult in the north. Besides, some of the children live in the villages there. Life tends to be difficult for the people there. Their parents can't make ends meet. However, there are some job openings here. For those children who are out of school, life could be very difficult for the children. When we go home—those of us who live here in the South and have some sources of income—when you go, their parents could ask you to bring them with you because they might not be able to take care of the children. They would ask you to go with their children and look for somebody for them to live with so that they, when they go back, they may have acquired a few belongings that would make them look good. That's why we bring them when we go.

Ali did not start recruiting because a neighbor or friend requested him to. Rather, parents wanted him to help their children migrate to the South to look for jobs and to learn some skills. Like the other non-formal recruiters he did not charge for his recruiting services. However, employers were at times responsible for his travel expenses. What differentiated him from the other non-formal recruiters was his habit of occasionally giving money to the parents of his recruits; not as payment for buying the children, but as emphasized, a way of sympathizing with them. As I understood it, he only wanted to be generous towards them. Such parents still maintained the right to go for their children whenever they wanted.

At the time of the interview he had been a recruiter for about 10 years. He travels to the north at least once every year and brings no less than two children with him on every visit. The youngest of his recruits was employed at 10. Most of them, he told me, were at least 12 years old. The average number of years that they remain continuously in servitude was between two and three years. Like Derrick and Sophia, his recruits look up to him as a surrogate parent. They report their problems to him. He usually mediates between recruits and their employers and transfers them to other employers if he deems it necessary.

Ahmed: The Non-Formal Recruiter at Bonyere. Ahmed also came to the south in search of a job through a former recruit. He worked as a watchman and farmer at Bonyere, which is even more rural than Tikobo #1. He was particularly scared of the interview. As a result, when he finally met me (I had previously visited the village twice without meeting him.), he walked me two to three miles to his employer's house to introduce me to them and to give them the chance to assess me. I had no idea why we had to meet his employers until we got there. The male employer was not available. I spoke to his wife about my research. This woman called her son, a high school drop-out, to talk to me and to evaluate the truth in what I had told them about me and the research. Some of Ali's responses had alerted me to the possibility of some recruiters refusing to answer my questions or to grant the interview because of the fear that I could be a government investigator. I showed him my business card in an attempt to convince him that I was not working for the Government of Ghana.

Looking at the expression on the boy's face, I assumed he would not recommend that Ahmed gave the interview, thus I thanked them for their time and set out to leave. A couple of minutes later, I saw Ahmed running after me. He said that he had been given the go-ahead to grant the interview and explained that he was not only concerned about himself but about my safety too. He told me that only three weeks earlier, three strangers had been killed under circumstances that were similar to my visit. He also said that another stranger who had requested the assistance of a small girl lured her to the outskirts of the village and had her killed. The next day when the girl's body was found, parts of it had been cut off, possibly for voodoo rituals.

I spoke to one servant that Ahmed had recruited. She was manning a convenience store at the market at Tikobo #1. This recruit, Hawa, could not tell me her age, but looked younger than 10. Her employer told me she was eight and had been living with her as a domestic servant for two years and two months. Ahmed is her paternal uncle. This particular girl's employer had asked around for domestic servants and had been directed to Ahmed. Usually, Ahmed would have taken money for transportation to go to the north for a child. However, his brother, Hawa's father, who had already migrated to Ashanti Region in the south, was also looking for an employer for this child. Hawa was thus sent to live with her current employer at Tikobo #1. It was through Hawa and her employer that I located Ahmed.

Ahmed confirmed he had recruited two girls for his employer. While waiting for him on my first visit, I learned from his child that when he went home a couple of months earlier, he brought two children back with him. Like Ali and the other non-formal recruiters, Ahmed told me he never got paid for his services as a recruiter and also remained constantly in touch with his recruits.

All four non-formal recruiters told me that they were happy to help both domestic servants and the employing households. There was no way I could prove them wrong. However, I observed that Derrick derived some level of satisfaction and pride in being an associate of the elite households for which he recruited children. His statements about the backgrounds of his clients and the way parents approached him whenever he visited his hometown, a village, most likely put him on a level that surpassed any monetary benefits he would gain if they paid him for his recruiting duties. Ali and Ahmed did not know each other although they both came from the northernmost part of the country and lived only a 10 minute drive from each other. Nevertheless, their explanations of why they brought children from their villages corroborated each other's statements. They told me in separate interviews that their concerns about the poor children in their respective home-towns drove them to become recruiters.

While all these non-formal agents of recruitment played the role of surrogate parents, voluntarily recruited children for employers, and received hardly any pay for their services, I observed some significant differences between Ahmed's and Ali's recruits and those of Derrick's and Sophia's. Unlike Derrick's and Sophia's, Ali's and Ahmed's recruits live in less developed towns. They mostly lived with petty traders who did not need them to work only around the house but also to hawk wares and keep their small shops for them. Although one of Sophia's re-cruits sold pastries for her employer, a teacher whose husband taught at a univer-sity, petty trading by domestic servants for their employers is not as prevalent in the major cities as they are in semi-urban communities.

Another difference is the educational backgrounds and economic positions of the employers with whom these recruits live. Whereas employers at Tikobo #1 and Bonyere are primarily semi-educated or uneducated low income earners who live off petty trading, those at Accra and Cape Coast that Derrick and Sophia served are highly educated university professors and businessmen who have bet-ter economic standing and social class than Ali's and Ahmed's clients.

I also observed a low turnover among Ali's and Ahmed's recruits. One factor probably responsible for this is the levels of poverty in their respective home-towns. Ahmed and Ali recruit boys and girls from the North. My observation cor-roborates traditional views that Northern Ghanaians are most subservient among all the tribal groups in Ghana. Additionally, the domestic servants from that part of the country seemed more committed than those from other parts of the country. This is probably due to the fact that Northern Ghana is the poorest of all the re-gions. Map II on the incidence of poverty in Ghana shows that the three northern regions, i.e. Northern Region, Upper East and Upper West Regions are the poor-est. Given their desperation to escape severe levels of poverty, they more easily tolerate those abuses characteristic of domestic servitude in general, which the girls from the south cannot endure for long.

Another factor is the similarities between their hometowns and the villages in which they served. As home to the poorest regions in the country, the northern part of Ghana is the least developed and thus exhibits much of the rural attri-butes that characterize Tikobo #1 and Bonyere. Among these characteristics is the level of communalism that domestic servants at Accra, Kumasi and Cape Coast lacked. In the villages, these domestic servants experienced what might qualify as mechanical solidarity, to borrow Emile Durkheim's concept. Based primarily on shared expectations and norms, life in the village is communal and simple. Living much like one big family in times of need, individuals are able to rely on fellow villagers for assistance without immediate reciprocal exchanges. Conversely, life in the cities is the direct opposite, where few seem to care about each other un-less personal relationships have been established. Contrary to their rural cultures, domestic servants cannot be friendly to everybody that they meet in the cities and thus feel as though they are living in cages. Some recruits to Accra, Cape Coast, or Kumasi complain of the quiet and individualistic nature of their neighborhoods and abrogate their contracts as a result.

Closely related to the above is the third factor; lack of competitiveness in the rural areas. In the village and semi-urban communities, servants feel more at home. This is not the same in the cities where most servants have to live the lives of outsiders, not being able to access basic household resources and space like actual family members. This, coupled with the communal nature of the less individualistic nature of the semi-urban communities into which they are recruited, makes it easier for them to stay longer there than in the cities.

To conclude this discussion on the processes of recruitment, it is worthy to note that whatever means through which servants are recruited, the probability of staying in touch with one's own family or recruiter is higher than not. Out of the 58 current and former domestic servants interviewed, only three could not remain in touch with either their family members or recruiters. Two of the three servants, Selasie and Molly, were recruited between the ages of two and three and so could not recall how to locate their families. Selasie was still in servitude at the time of this research. At 13 years of age, she had stayed in servitude for at least 10 years and so knew nothing about her own family. Molly got the chance to be with her mother a few years after servitude and after a couple of visits was not allowed to go back to servitude. The third servant is Claudia. She was old enough to identify her parents but did not know how to get to her house at Tema, a metropolitan town located near Accra.

NATURE AND STRUCTURE OF RELATIONSHIPS BETWEEN EMPLOYERS AND DOMESTIC SERVANTS

In the previous sub-sections, I described the role that relative and non-relative recruiters play in the employment processes of domestic servants. A major observation that I made from these processes is the fact that unless employed through formal agencies, domestic servants or their families always retain some connections with the recruiters or their employers. In addition, I observed three different patterns of relationships among recruiters, employers, and domestic servants and their families. I refer to these as the non-familial relationship, the kin-group relationship and the shared-solidarity relationship. In the following paragraphs I discuss these different patterns of relationships and how they impact the treatment of domestic servants by their employers and vice versa.

Non-Familial Relationships

The pattern of non-familial relationship exists where domestic servants work for total strangers who come from and live in different parts of the country. Such employers go through any of the three processes of recruitment to obtain their domestic servants. The domestic servants that I knew, while growing up, lived in households where they had no kin ties and were not from the same hometowns as their employers. This dominance of children working for families that they were not related to is true for the participants in this study. The largest number of my respondents fell under this category of non-familiar relationship. As many as 25 of the 44 current domestic servants and nine of the 14 former domestic servants lived with people with whom they were not in any way related. Three of the 25 current domestic servants and two former domestic servants came from the same hometowns as their employers; the type of relationship existing between them and their employers is outlined below.

As already suggested, none of the domestic servants in this research lived with other households for altruistic reasons. The only persons who could be exempted from this assertion are Selasie and Molly who were recruited between the tender ages of two and three. Selasie, for instance, did not know why or how she came to live with her employer. All the others, including eight-year-old Hawa, knew that they were there either to be able to go to school or to be able to learn a trade after a specified period of service. Therefore, the 39 domestic servants who shared non-familial relationships with their employers either volunteered or accepted the offer to live in these strange households expecting that they would receive remuneration for their services.

Given that they were not related to their employers, one would expect that the latter would understand the children's reasons for accepting the role of providing services and to keep their part of the contract. In this category, this was not the case with a majority of the domestic servants whom I interviewed. If there was any understanding of the children's plight on the part of their employers, it would have been in regards to the desperateness of the children's struggle to live with other families in order to accumulate funds and other resources towards their skill training. That desperation, I assume, led these non-relative employers to prolong the children's stay with them because of the anticipation that most of them would fear abrogating their contracts and forfeiting their accumulated incomes. Besides Lily, Selasie, and Hawa and five of the older cohorts of former domestic servants who were very young at the time of their recruitment and so could not specify the number of years that they would like to stay in servitude, all the other domestic servants expected to be paid off at the end of their second year unless they received regular payments at the end of every month. They, however, stayed longer than two years.

Although parents and/or informal or non-formal recruiters often knew where domestic servants lived regardless of the kind of relationship and thus could communicate with them and their employers, none of them ever interceded to ensure that employers keep their promises. Often, parents did not have direct contacts with their domestic servant children. This, however, was not the case for recruiters. Derrick, Sophia, Ali, and Ahmed stayed in regular touch with their recruits. They told me that this was to make sure that the children were doing fine in servitude. Nevertheless, the interviews did not evidence any instance where they requested that employers enrolled their servants in training because the agreed period of two or three years had elapsed.

When living with unrelated families, domestic servants recruited through non-formal processes stood the risk of overstaying their contract period if they wanted to be enrolled into the chosen skill training, the surrogate parenthood of non-formal recruiters notwithstanding. In this research, there were six current domestic servants who were recruited through non-formal processes to live with strangers. One of them was Sophia's recruit who received a monthly wage as arranged. Mansah, one of Derrick's recruits whom I interviewed, was paid, but only when she decided to leave for wrongful accusation. Derrick told me he usually arranged with employers to keep the servants' pay until they were ready to leave, so Mansah receiving her pay at the time of her departure was not abnormal. Although he claimed to ensure that his recruits were remunerated regularly, the other two servants that I encountered during this research never received any pay. As Chapter Six illustrates, Michael and his colleague domestic servant did not arrange to receive regular payments at the end of the month. Given the employer's sexual harassment of the girl, she ran away without getting paid. Michael also left because his employer suspected that he had connived with the girl in her escape. This employer was no longer cheerful towards him, and as a result, this male servant also ran away without pay.

Hawa was recruited by her uncle to live with a stranger. In interviews with this uncle and her employer, I learned that she would be enrolled in an apprentice training when she came of age. She was only eight at the time of this interview and had already spent two years in servitude. When I interviewed one of Ali's recruits, he was preparing to send her back because her parents had requested that she return home. She did not receive any pay for her services and did not indicate why she was not paid. My enquiries from Ahmed indicated that he would collect the pay and send it to her later.

Servants in this category who were recruited through informal processes relative to those employed through non-formal processes were at a higher risk of exploitation. While it is not disputable that their parents knew who to contact in case they wanted to stay in touch with their children in servitude, there was no sign of them ever contacting the employers about their children's pay. Consequently, informally recruited domestic servants who stayed with strangers waited the longest to either leave servitude or to be enrolled into domestic servitude. Hawa's employer had another domestic servant, an older person, who was recruited at the age of eight. At the time of this interview, she had been living with her employer for eight years. This employer stated in the interview that this other servant had been employed through informal means and that she was preparing to send her away. Despite her suggestion of paying her off in a very generous manner, I observed that the length of time that this girl had stayed in servitude probably made that claim of generosity questionable.

Unlike those recruited by non-formal agents, domestic servants who were appointed through informal means usually lost their accumulated incomes if they decided to leave without agreeing on a departure date with their employers. Often they ran away. Below is a description by an employer explaining how she sent off a servant who decided to leave because the area was too quiet and individualistic and thus lacked the type of mechanical cohesion she was accustomed to in her village:

> ...So the woman [an informal recruiter] rang me and told me that the girl is there. I should ... not to give her money to her because she, she the woman gave transport to bring her here, and the transport is I think 20,000 or so... So I should deduct that 20,000 from the payment. At that time I was paying her 30,000; that is I think about three years ago. So I should deduct that money and then give the rest to her. So I took the woman's money, even the woman sent her maidservant to come and collect her money when they were coming. So I gave the rest to her, and she left ... So I collected all the things my daughter gave to her, I took it. I didn't give it to her. Even what she was wearing from top to slippers is mine. I took everything, because you haven't stayed here even for three months.

Employers' displeasure at the sudden departure of their servants notwithstanding, some servants received partial compensation for their services. The servants received such payments if their families consulted with the employers about the payment. Doreen, 19, was living with her third employer at the time of this study. She told me that her current employers promised to let her start some type of skill training soon after her recruitment. When I spoke to the female employer she told me otherwise. According to her, Doreen was going to be enrolled to become a hairdressing apprentice after two to three years. Nevertheless, Doreen was planning to leave at the end of two years if she had not started by then. She was forced to return to her parents when her first employer, a hairdresser who was training her at the time, decided to relocate in another town for personal reasons. The second family promised to help her continue with her training in hairdressing but instead made her sell bread and water in addition to performing household chores.

Eight months into her stay with them, her employer's husband attempted to assault her sexually. Doreen had been raped before, and because of that experience, she decided to run away without informing anybody in her current employer's household. When her family returned to discuss her pay with the employing household, this family came up with a figure that was supposed to be paid her every day, and from that, they made deductions for her breakfast, lunch, and supper and for medical expenses. As she said, the amount of money left was so meager she decided to never step a foot in that house again to say hello to them should she ever visit that neighborhood.

The on-going discussions in this section illustrate the manner in which the participants in this research were exploited—when they lived with total strangers—non-relatives who did not come from their villages or hometowns. We observe their exploitation occurring through the length of time that they were required to stay before pay and through their remuneration. Although it is beneficial for some girls to live in servitude because they are able to learn a trade as a result, the extent of exploitation and humiliation that they go through might counteract these benefits. In the next subsection, we note that children who live with relatives suffer the same level of humiliation and exploitation.

Kin-Group Relationships

The relationship existing between a domestic servant and her employer is categorized as kin group if they are related by blood or through marriage. The incidence of children living with older members in their extended families actually started this trend of domestic servitude in Ghana, according to the Director of Ghana's Department of Social Welfare, Mrs. Mary Amadu, one of the two government officials whom I interviewed in the course of this research. Mrs. Amadu attributed domestic servitude in Ghana to the historical pattern of extended families allowing one of their younger female members to migrate with another member to a distant area in order to help her with domestic services. Reciprocally, the older family member was to provide the helper with free formal education and training in housekeeping. While this helped the domestic servant to acquire formal education and gender-related skills, the family back home was spared the trouble of taking care of another member. Some of the older women with whom I spoke prior to this research as well as those who participated in the research confirmed the level of discrimination and exploitation that children living with extended family members had to endure while in servitude.

Out of 44 current domestic servants, seven lived with blood relations. There was one male among them. Five former domestic servants also lived with their own relatives. My pre-research expectation that domestic servants currently living with relatives would be least abused proved to be wrong for the respondents in this research. Complaints of abuses seemed to be more dominant among domestic servants who lived with their own relatives; on average, they also stayed much longer than those who lived with non-relatives.

Like the other domestic servants, those who lived with blood relations complained of two things, verbal and/or physical abuse and the lack of remuneration for their services. Their expectations of being enrolled in good private schools, S.S.S., or even be given the chance to learn trades as promised by their relative-employers were either never realized or took too long to actualize. In Michael's household, for instance, there was a third domestic servant who was related to their employer. I nicknamed him James. At the time of this research James had lived with his cousin for eight years. He said his father sent him to this house so he could further his education at the S.S.S. level. He was there the first time, but there were about four servants. Hence, his cousin asked him to go away for some time. A couple of months later, the cousin sent for him. He was elated at the invitation, thinking that he was going to be enrolled in school. For the next five years, he provided domestic services and took care of the lawn and the house. It was his cousin's new wife, who, soon after joining the household sympathized with James' situation and consequently registered him as an apprentice in a tailor's shop. Faced with the difficulties of buying his own supplies for sewing practice as well as transportation to and from the tailoring shop, James finally decided to leave his cousin's house so he could sew on the side to make money. In a telephone conversation with him in 2004, he told me he had to leave his cousin's place because he had virtually stopped taking care of him financially.

Samira and Patricia also lived with some relatives. Patricia lived with her cousin at age 10. For close to 11 years, she provided domestic services but received nothing when her cousin asked her to leave. Samira lived with two relatives, and when she had to leave, she received nothing from either employer. Although both of them went to school, the number of hours they worked around the house or engaged in economic activities prevented them from performing satisfactorily in school. At the time of this research, Samira was about to graduate from a vocational training school. She was learning to become a fashion designer. Her mother was taking care of her at the time.

Like Samira and Patricia, most of the domestic servants who lived with relatives in Accra did not have life and working conditions any better than those who lived with non-relatives. Their employers were primarily concerned with the gains they made from these young women. I found Mary, another such victim, at a shop in Teshie Nungua Estates. When I explained the purpose of the research and requested her consent for me to interview her, she directed me to an older woman whom I estimated to be in her mid-thirties, to ask for permission. Mary helped me with a stool and grabbed one for herself when the lady who is supposed to be her niece gave her the go-ahead to grant the interview. She wept throughout the interview and kept turning and looking around. It was apparent that she was apprehensive about something, but I had no way of knowing that she had to go home for household chores around this time and was trying to avoid being seen by her cousin who was also her employer. About half-way through the interview, a car stopped in front of the shop. Without saying a word to me, Mary jumped out of her seat and rushed to the car. I thought she was going to help a customer and so paused the recorder and waited. Soon, I saw her get in the car, which drove away immediately. I passed by the shop a couple of times to see if I could get her to complete the interview. Although her employer's daughter gave me the initial permission to interview her, I did not go in to ask of her again for fear she could be penalized. Thus Mary's employer's background is unknown.

As far as sexual harassment is concerned, only Doreen encountered it while living with her aunt. This occurred before she worked for non-relatives. The details of this assault are given under the subsection on why domestic servants prematurely leave servitude.

Shared-Solidarity Relationships

The shared-solidarity relationship exists when domestic servants and their employers come from the same village or hometown but are not related by blood or through marriage. There were ten respondents who came from the same hometowns as the female heads (i.e. the wives of the male heads) of the households that they lived in. Only one former domestic servant came from the same hometown as a male employer. The female heads are always directly responsible for the domestic servants. With the exception of two cases, females usually arranged for servants to be recruited, gave them some type of informal orientation, and supervised their work. This was true in all types of recruitment and relationship.

In these interviews I discovered how a family could maintain cordial and warm relationship with its domestic servants as a result of altruistic moral obligations simply by coming from the same hometowns as the servants, while others, in contrast, focused more on self-interest benefits derived from their servants and thus could not tolerate their poor services. I assumed that although the quest for cheap labor drew families to rely on informal means of recruitment and thus on the vulnerable positions of their hometown girls, the bond existing between the two groups coming from the same village also played a part in the relationship between these employers and their servants. I observed also that animosity usually existing between domestic servants and employers who came from same hometown as theirs is less intense than that found in others. There were exceptional cases though, one being the relationship between Emelia and her employer.

Two households at Cape Coast lived with domestic servants who came from the wives' hometowns. Mrs. Biney, one of the two employers, showed the least differentiation between her own family and her domestic servants. I was able to interview her and two of her domestic servants, Rita and Cynthia. She usually allowed her domestic servants to receive training in her hairdressing salon. Most of her domestic servants came from her hometown in the Western Region. As she pointed out, this connection served as the basis of her positive attitude towards her domestic servants. When she decided to no longer obtain young women from her hometown because of disrespectful behavior by some of them, she continued to exhibit similar commitment to the girls that she recruited from other villages. At the time of the interview, she lived with three girls, one of whom was her sister's daughter, and another, a distant relation.

Serwah is another domestic servant who lived with a hometown person. Like Mrs. Biney's family, Serwah's employer had another domestic servant, but from a different village. Although Serwah was pleased with her status as a domestic servant in the city, her employer could not express similar sentiments about her. In an interview with this employer, I learned that Serwah was not as smart and efficient as the other domestic servant who had lived in this household for over five years. This employer's dissatisfaction notwithstanding, she remained equally polite and generous to both of them; most likely because of the hometown connection she shared with Serwah.

Unfortunately, the third respondent who lived with a hometown family, Emelia, did not enjoy the sort of cordial relationship that existed in Mrs. Biney's and Serwah's households. It was sad listening to some of her experiences in her current employer's household, although she appeared to be the strongest willed respondent in this research. At sixteen, she was living with her third employer. Both the second and third had come from the same hometown as she. She willingly left the first employer when she was accused of having had a boyfriend. She, however, told me that she wished she could go back to that city and to do the same work—selling secondhand clothing—although not necessarily with the same employer. She received ill-treatment from her current employer as well as the latter's three children. Usually, the employer was impatient whenever an argument ensued between the domestic servant and the children. The employer would not listen to this respondent's side of the story but would jump to unfounded conclusions that usually resulted in the employer meting out some sort of punishment to the servant, which were at times mere insults.

While interviewing this employer I noted that most of the allegations made against her by domestic servants were valid. She was one among many employers who demonstrated in their responses their belief that domestic servants had to be maltreated or made to feel subservient to the rest of the family. For example, she did not care when her children misbehaved towards her domestic servants. Her choice of words used to describe her domestic servants was also demeaning. In all my visits to this family, I noted that neither the children nor the mother was friendly towards the domestic servant.

This employer said she preferred girls from her village because of the passion and love she has for that community. In her opinion, these girls were mostly underprivileged, and one way of helping to alleviate their plight was to bring them to the city and when they left at least give them a sewing machine. Usually, she promised to enroll them in skill training after a two-year stay with her. In case she decided to send them away for dissatisfactory services, in which case the girls do not stay throughout the agreed period, her commitment to the girls from her village moved her to see them off on a good note, at least getting them the sewing machine. Her second domestic servant lived with her for five years. It was in the fifth year that this girl started training in dressmaking. Unfortunately, this employer suspected she had started dating and so sent her away. For her reward, this previous domestic servant received a sewing machine and some cash to pay part of her reenrollment into training.

Emelia lived with this employer nearly a year, and the employer was making preparations to send her back to the village. I noted that this employer had a high house-help turnover and a pattern emerged; there was the tendency for her and the rest of the family to be welcoming and tolerant the first few months of a helper's stay with them, but then soon afterwards, when the novelty wore off, petty mistakes on the part of the helper upset her. Consequently, she would either hit the helper or utter certain derogatory remarks that would cause the servants to feel uncomfortable, out of place, and nostalgic. When asked what problems she had with the servants, Emelia's employer stated that

> One of them was a thief. She wasn't cheerful, she was always moody. The second one also stole a little bit. Some of them used to beat my children. They yelled at them. You buy your lactogen and they ate it, so you had to buy more than you needed so you will always have some for your children. This one specially has problem with boys. By the time you come back, she would have locked the door and left for her boyfriend. Send her to go for this [pointing to her son] from school, she will go with her boyfriend and ask him to stay outside and wait for her. When you leave, she makes so many phone calls, to a boy behind this building. If you ask her to do anything, she doesn't do it. She doesn't use her initiative and when you tell her, she doesn't do it.

In conclusion, Chapter IV outlines the nature and type of relationships that exist between domestic servants and their employers. Domestic servants suffer abuses and exploitation in all three types of relationships. Nevertheless, girls who lived with their relatives gave the impressions of suffering the worst exploitation and abuses in this study. They had to stay longer than normal before any training, and if they left on a bad note, they were denied any payment due them. Girls who came from same hometowns as their employers had a higher chance of developing a satisfactory relationship with their employing households. I assumed that such employers felt it a moral obligation to be honest in their dealings with their hometown girls, although the domestic servants in this type of relationship were not always allowed to learn a trade within the agreed upon time frame.

CHAPTER SUMMARY AND CONCLUSION

This research discovers three processes of recruitment, namely formal, non-formal, and informal processes. The interviews reveal that domestic servants who are recruited through the formal processes are usually older than the minimum working age and they usually complete the basic education before accepting such offers. Some of the servants recruited through non-formal processes complete the basic education but are usually younger than 18. Unless their recruiters and families make prior arrangements with their employers to pay them regularly, they may have to wait until the end of the agreed period of service to get paid. However, if the servant decided to leave before that period, she may lose the accumulated income. Unlike these two categories of domestic servants, those recruited through informal processes usually live with relatives or non-relatives with whom their families have some degree of contact. These are more likely to be exploited and to stay longer before receiving payment for their service.

The processes of recruitment that this research observes among the participants are not enslaving. In all three forms of recruitment, I observed that children exercise the right of participating in the decisions regarding their enrollment into domestic servitude although they believe that their parents should have the last say. Contrary to what exists in other societies, the domestic servants who responded to this research were relatively mature and knowledgeable enough to understand the demands of their responsibilities. They understand the financial constraints facing their parents and the fact that child domestic servitude is probably the only avenue through which they would ever receive the training that they expect.

The only exceptions were those current and former domestic servants who were recruited between 3 and 12 years of age and so did not understand the purpose and implications of their servitude or simply because they were below the minimum working age, that is if we consider the age permitting children to work in light industry is 13. Such servants were more likely to have dropped out of school or were never enrolled at all. If they stayed longer without contact with their biological families, they may not be able to trace their way back home should it become necessary for them to.

Chapter V

CULTURE OF GHANA AND ITS IMPACT ON CHILD DOMESTICS

The literature suggests that three interrelated factors define and determine the chances for opportunities of women in Africa and Ghana in particular. There are indigenous gender structures: lack of women's access to credit and capital and economic growth and development policies. In previous sections I discussed existing reports on development programs and how they negatively affect the lives of Ghanaians in general. Other research focused on the impact of neo-liberal economic policies which, while interacting with existing traditional gender structures and norms, neglected women's economic roles and thus intensified their lack of access to vital socioeconomic resources. These gender and economic structures subordinating women's statuses in some Ghanaian cultures to those of men make it easier for girls to be exploited within the household as domestic servants.

Although these structures do not directly prevent girls from accessing formal education, their willingness to accept offers of domestic servitude partially depends on them. In my research I discovered that girls accept work as domestic servants because they expect to learn gender related roles. Additionally, employers and recruiters in this study demonstrated that the latter prefer to hire girls as servants because of the gender-related chores they assign to them. As Chapter Six shows, another reason that girls end up in domestic servitude is due to their parents' inability to finance their high school education. In this chapter, I discuss the literature on gender constructions inherent in patterns of lineage in Ghana and outline their relationship to child domestic servitude as are observable in my research.

Gender is "the constellation of rules and identities that prescribe behavior for persons, in their social roles as men and women" (Kevane, 2004: 1). Every society has its characteristic gender traits (Kevane, 2004). Some core values of these traits survive external pressures and remain relatively stable over a significant period. Core values governing inheritance and succession in Ghana, for example, have seen very little change. These values demonstrate unequal power distribution among males and females. However, some scholars—including Oyeronke Oyewumi (1997), Ifi Amadiume (1987) and Sean Hawkins (2002)—attribute certain aspects of African gender structures to processes of colonization. Although arguments invalidating this assertion are beyond the scope of this book, it can be observed that elements of pre-colonial gender structures that have outlived sociocultural changes in Ghana also impact socialization of children and the induction of girls into domestic servitude.

LINEAGE AND GENDER STRUCTURES IN GHANA

While it is not disputable that there is a misrepresentation of African women in some Western gender and feminist discourse as the scholars mentioned above argue, patterns of descent in those African countries where these scholars researched exhibit pre-colonial discriminatory gender structures that were tilted against women and which interacted with emergent colonial structures to create the category of disadvantaged women whom we witness today in African cultures. Gender structures in African countries derive from traditional systems of descent that define rights of inheritance and succession. These patterns are usually matrilineal or patrilineal. In matrilineal societies all males and females trace their descent through a female line, from a common ancestry (Nukunya, 1992; Stoeltje, 1995). Jeanne K. Henn (1984) defines it as "the practice of tracing kinship allegiance and inheritance rights through the mother's family" (Henn, 1984: 8). In this system, a woman's brother with whom she shares the same mother is responsible for her children. Both males and females whose biological fathers belong to a particular matrilineal group cannot inherit or succeed anybody within that group. Usually, the lineage has a head (the Abusua Panin). This head has to belong to the family matrilineally and must always be a male (Nukunya, 1992). The only exception exists in Mpohor Wassa District of the Western Region where two women have been made chiefs rather than queen mothers as is the norm in other traditional areas.

In Ghana, the Akan-speaking peoples of Ashanti, Akim, Akwapim, Brong, Fante, and Ahanta ethnic groups are matrilineal (Nukunya, 1992). An estimated 49% of the research population is matrilineal (Ghana Home Page, 2005), although in the rest of Africa patrilineal systems outnumber matriliny by far (Nukunya, 1992).

Political power in matrilineal families is usually the antithesis of what exists within patrilineages. Women in patrilineal societies are relatively less powerful than their counterparts in matrilineal groups. In this system, males and females trace their lineage through a male line to a common ancestor. Unlike matrilineal relationships, fathers are responsible for their own children (Nukunya, 1992). In their absence, their children become the responsibility of their paternal brothers who are considered traditionally eligible for inheritance. In Ghana, the Ewe, the Ga, the Adangme, the Kusasi, the Gonja, Dagomba, Kokomba, and Mamprusi ethnic groups are patrilineal. The Yoruba of Nigeria, which Oyewumi researched, are also patrilineal.

While conventional knowledge asserts that matrilineal systems vest more power in females than males, rules of inheritance, widowhood rites, and traditional political systems empower males in both matrilineal and patrilineal systems, thus making females the subservient category in either system. The rules of inheritance and succession are intertwined with those of widowhood and its rituals, rites of marriage, and traditional political systems to make women less powerful, generally.

The matrilineal woman's acclaimed power, although true relative to their counterparts in patriliny, stems from and probably rests with their biological relationship to their children. Given that persons who are eligible for succession and inheritance in matrilineal systems must trace their ancestry biologically through their mothers, the woman's role in the family's certainty of their blood relatives is, inarguably, an immense one. The importance of the matrilineal mother's role is indispensable especially in the absence of advanced scientific methods such as DNA testing to certify maternity or paternity. In fact oral history has it that Akan royal households preferred matriliny because of the higher probability of being certain of the mother's biological relationship to her child, which is not the same for that existing between fathers and their offspring. Akan groups believe that the woman's biological link to her children is fully guaranteed, while the father's blood relationship with his children could be questioned. In view of this, the chiefs, kings, queen-mothers, and all persons occupying prominent traditional positions have always been selected based on their maternal relationship to the family.

Matrilineal women enjoy another important role of power, albeit one restricted to those from royal households and who end up as queen-mothers. The queen-mother is privileged to be the only person who could select the king or the chief. This power is, however, limited by the whims of an all male king-making sub-committee who could place impediments in her way, by finding faults with and rejecting the person she chooses. Beyond the queen-mother's privilege of selecting the prospective chief or king for vetting by the more superior king-making sub-committee, she has no power over the chief. She is as much a subject of the chief as any other member of the community. This shows that even in matrilineal groups, the woman's political power is subordinated to that of males. That state of subordination is manifested in taboos that prevent the queen-mother and all other women from entering some palace shrines and from entering the palace during her /their menstrual period/s.

Processes of traditional marriage also vest more power in men than in women. This is observed in the important roles that maternal uncles, rather than mothers, play in the marriage rites of their maternal sisters' children. Uncles usually oversee marriages of these nieces to serve as liaison between his family (and that of the bride-to-be) and the groom and his family. The Akan traditional marriage, for instance, entails different stages, and at each stage the husband-to-be presents gifts to the bride's family and her father (Nukunya, 1992; Tashjion & Allman, 2002), usually through the bride's uncles. The mother through whom the bride is a legitimate member of the lineage is only assigned roles that are relatively less important and requiring no leadership skills. She and other female elders of the kinship group counsel the bride about feminine and passive female roles in marriages.

Matriliny and patriliny also define separate patterns of residence for married couples, although married couples utilize both maternal and paternal ties in their household organizations and patterns of residence (Nukunya, 1992). Historically, patrilineal societies have had more specified residential patterns. They were usually patrilocal. Under this system, married couples had to live in the husband's father's home (Nukunya, 1992). The pattern of residence could also be duolocal, in which case the couple lived in separate homes. This existed among the Ga people of Accra, Ghana. Residential patterns are not so distinct among matrilineal groups. Some of them are patrilocal and since this contradicts matrilineal values, children belonging to such couples may have to live with their mother's family (Nukunya, 1992).

Women who marry into patrilineal families are considered strangers (Nukunya, 1992) and for that matter are less powerful relative to the men in these groups. Husbands exercise the right of using their wives' labor (Nukunya, 1992; Hawkins, 2002) and thus derive invaluable productive and reproductive benefits from them. Women in pre-colonial patrilineal systems served as a source of labor for their husbands (Henn, 1984; Coquery-Vidrovitch, 1997). As Godwin K. Nukunya (1992) suggests, "... in a patrilineal society, a married woman bears children for her husband's lineage" (Nukunya, 1992: 43).

In most of pre-colonial Africa, labor, rather than land, was scarcest of all the factors of production. Hence, husbands from either matrilineal or patrilineal ethnic groups relied on their wives' labor and those of their children for work on their fields (Henn, 1984: 5). It is against this background that some scholars attribute the emergence of polygyny to women's productive role on their husband's field and their reproductive role, which ensure that there is a pool of free labor supply for males (Coquery-Vidrovitch, 1997; Henn, 1984). As Catherine Cockquery (1997) succinctly states, "for the family receiving, whether birth family or future in laws, a girl was a source of wealth—a promise of work and a guarantee of children" (10).

Besides farm labor, women had to provide domestic services that included fetching water from the stream, cooking, cleaning, and looking after the children (Tashjian and Allman, 2002). In exchange for her services, the husband provided care and maintenance for their wives. They provided meat, clothing, and food (Tashjion and Allman, 2002).

Today, the husband's advantaged position over his spouse is slowly dwindling because of

> ...comparative resources which husband and wife bring to marriage, such as education and income and the type of occupational and kinship positions each maintains outside the conjugal family, as well as by the prescribed and traditional authority patterns of the cultures to which they belong (Oppong, 1974: 115).

Christine Oppong (1974) states further that "wherever women have access to strategic resources, being important economic producers and managers of property, their part in domestic decision-making has been shown in numerous studies to be potentially enhanced "(Oppong, 1974: 115). Unfortunately, women's lack of access to information, capital, private savings, and their underprivileged statuses in terms of educational opportunities and attainment, as outlined earlier, make the dwindling in male powers slower if not impossible for many poor women in both rural and urban regions.

Most of the need for female labor on farms existed in rural regions. Nevertheless, these persistent gender structures determined the kind of work that they did in pre-colonial and colonial cities (Guyer, 1984: 35). As suggested earlier, these structures continue to thwart women's development in many low income countries. "Only a few women have been able to overcome the socioeconomic constraints that keep women illiterate, poorly paid, or marginally self-employed" (Guyer, 1984: 35). The only contribution that colonization made to that, which in itself was enormous, is the monetization of African economies. Some farm produce was converted into cash crops, and men dominated their cultivation. If what Oyewumi, Amadiume and the others suggest is correct, then it is in terms of gender-related changes that occurred through the monetization of African economies. Men had more access to wage labor and to the production of cash crops. The impact of such privileges has continued until today in some cultures.

The bulk of the changes resulting from colonization occurred through monetization of the economies in Africa. Colonization introduced cash crops such as cocoa and coffee to many Sub-Saharan African countries. Although women and men cultivated some crops for household consumption prior to that period, this changed with the onset of cash cropping. Land needed for food crop cultivation was switched for cash cropping. Men became responsible for cash crops, while women concentrated on food crops (Coquery-Vidrovitch, 1997; Guyer, 1984). Among the Brongs of Ghana, for instance, both men and women cultivated cotton and indigo for household consumption until these became cash crops and consequently the specialization of men (Stahl and Cruz, 1998). Likewise, in the Ashanti Region lands originally used for food crops were diverted for cocoa production and thus the specialization of men. Women became the economic and social dependents of men while they remained responsible for the cultivation of food crops for their household's consumption (Henn, 1984).

When fertile lands for cash and food cropping were exhausted, Ashanti men migrated to the Brong Ahafo, and Western Regions to further their cash crop production. Urbanization occurred around the same time, causing rural men to migrate to urban centers in search of wage labor. In order to force African males to desert their farms to work in European enterprises in the cities, property taxes were introduced in some African colonies by 1903 (White, 1984). Given that lands in some farming areas had become less fertile and also that these property taxes were not affordable by rural residents, males had to succumb to work in European enterprises in the cities. Doing so created vacuums within households, thus increasing the workload on women. Although women could be economically independent (Henn, 1984), unlike men, (Obbo, 1980; Coquery-Vidrovtch, 1997), colonial measures and missionary policies prevented them from migrating into the big cities in pursuit of paid occupations; as a result most women became household heads.

This burden has persisted to the present. The rural African woman's "labor day has seen very little change", as Henn suggests (Henn, 1984:1). In order to provide their families' basic food (Boserup, 1970; Henn, 1984; Guyer, 1984), most days they must work in the fields from four to eight hours, aided only by a simple hoe They must also work a second labor day fetching firewood and water, and drying, shelling, storing, and cooking the foods from their gardens, all the while caring for their children (Henn, 1984: 2). Therefore, they could not make the time to listen to agronomists or to receive the training that would enhance productive roles within the household. They could not go to school either. As a result, they could not get wage labor (Guyer, 1984) and besides work on farms, became self-employed. Women's authority in market trading was carried over into the post-colonial era, but the same constraints mentioned earlier have prevented a large number of them from expanding their businesses (Guyer, 1984).

RELATIONSHIP BETWEEN GENDER ROLE EXPECTATIONS AND CHILD DOMESTIC SERVITUDE

These historical attributes of gender relations and lineage in Ghana, to some extent, have connections to the employment of children in domestic servitude to-day. Although the lack of educational resources in rural regions negatively affect both boys and girls, the concentration of girls in domestic servitude reflects the tradition of girls being confined to the private sphere and women's poor conditions in rural regions. Among the respondents in this research, mothers, and in some cases fathers, look for opportunities that will promote better standards of living for their children. Both parents and children prefer that the latter avoid the problems of living in the rural area and working long hours in the fields and around the house. As I soon illustrate, both parents and children believe that living in the cities will not only help female children escape long hours of farming and walking long distances to fetch water and firewood in addition to other household chores, but will enable them to learn roles that will make them good mothers and wives. This subsection discusses the role of gender socialization, patterns of inheritance and succession, and other cultural practices relative to the incidence of child domestic servitude in Ghana.

As the Director of Ghana's Social Welfare, Mrs. Mary Amadu pointed out the primary reason that families allow their younger members to live with older relatives in the past was so that women and girls would be able to learn gender-related roles. As referenced earlier, she suggested that previously, families allowed their younger members to migrate with newly married relations in order to assist them with domestic chores. In return, the older relative put the younger girl through formal education, provided her with informal training in general etiquette, housekeeping skills, and the chance to learn a trade.

What the Director of Social Welfare told me corroborated my pre-research discussion with women who lived as domestic servants in the 1950s through the 1960s. I discovered, in fact, that they lived mostly with relatives. With the exception of Esther, the older cohorts of domestic servants lived with members of their extended families as "...that was the practice then," according to some of my respondents.

Responses by parents, employers, and domestic servants reflect the influence of gender constructions on contemporary child domestic servitude. They point to an interaction between gender role expectations, lack of funding, and educational resources to create domestic servitude among girls. If this were not the case, both boys and girls will be tracked into same activities when they are not able to enter senior secondary schools or to continue their education at the relevant levels.

Domestic servants asserted in the interviews that parents prefer their daughters to enter domestic servitude instead of their sons because of the nature of the responsibilities of domestics. A large number of them believe that they can learn good manners, as are defined by their cultures, while living in the cities. I felt this had nothing to do with the respondents' own wellbeing but that of their future husbands. At very young ages, they had already been socialized into being successful objects for their future husbands. They agreed that living in the cities would enhance their effectiveness in their objective positions as wives. As Akosua put it

> When you live with your parents, you are spoilt. When they send you, you can choose not to go. When you live with other families...when you live with

your mother and you work hard, you never find yourself wanting whenever you go to live somewhere else. If you work hard when living with other families, you will never find yourself wanting wherever you go. Besides, when you live with your mother, you won't live with her forever. A day will come when you will be married and be living in your husband's home. There, it won't be your mother who will be cooking for you then.

Serwah who was 15 at the time of my field research put it this way:

Some parents want their children to have some exposure. Some want their children to stay away from boys. There are those also who want their children to learn how to serve their husbands. They live in the villages and don't know what is going on. When they come here, they know what is going on, like being respectful, not calling people names.

Employers gave the same explanations for preferring girls, and added that to some extent, they were scared of the possibility of boys robbing them of their belongings or sexually abusing their young daughters. Only one employer confirmed knowing a household whose belongings were once stolen by a houseboy. Where households hired boys, this was usually in addition to domestic servants, and such boys were responsible for male-related gender roles like gardening, the care of livestock if any, washing vehicles, and doing the laundry for the male household heads. As mentioned in previous chapters, there were two male respondents in this research, and they were primarily responsible for these male roles.

Methods of payment of domestic servitude among older cohorts of domestic servants also point to the role of gender in the continued existence of this phenomenon in Ghana. Employers of domestic servants in the era before the 1980s usually performed initiation ceremonies in the form of puberty rites for their servants. At puberty, Ghanaian boys did not have to go through any special rituals. The girls, however, were subjected to yet another culture-specific socialization—the puberty rites, which are not organized as much as they used to in the period preceding the 1970s.

Puberty rites are special traditional ceremonies that were organized for girls to initiate them into adulthood and to honor them for not getting pregnant before their marriage. Historically, girls who became pregnant without having gone through this initiation ceremony and being duly married were banished from their communities. These traditions became relaxed in the 1970s, and today, it is hardly observed in most societies. Such initiation ceremonies differed from culture to culture among the research population.

Puberty rites for girls in the Ashanti Region began at dawn with a pouring of libation and preparation by the parents and members of the extended family to formally outdoor the girl in question. Throughout the day, the girl is adorned in expensive traditional clothing and seated on a traditional stool in an open yard to receive gifts and to listen to words of wisdom from well-wishers. At dusk, she is escorted to her room to begin a week of confinement. Throughout that period, the girl would receive training on motherhood, marriage, and about expectations of transitioning from childhood into adulthood. Today, no town or village in the Ashanti Region performs this ritual for its girls, most likely as a result of cultural diffusion, social change, and the influence of formal education on the status of the average Ghanaian woman. It is highly unlikely for educated women to consider this tradition relevant to their socio-cultural and economic development.

Given the cultural relevance attached to puberty rites for girls among the Ashantis I believe families of domestic servants found it sufficient for their girls to be provided the chance of going through this ceremony in lieu of cash payment for their services. Like the women I talked to before this research, the domestic servants of the pre-1980 era did not usually enter into agreements with their employers with regards to the method of payment, length of time required of them to serve, and how much they would be paid. They lived in servitude for as long as it took for them to get married. Before that, the relatives with whom they lived organized the puberty rites for them. As part of the puberty rites their employers presented them with kitchen utensils, traditional cloths, and other personal effects all of which are symbolic of female gender constructions.

Although these findings substantiate observations in the literature regarding the domination of girls in domestic servitude around the world, the data did not point to gender-related assertions that parents allowed their daughters into domestic servitude because of the belief that they would be secure there. Parents were more concerned about their daughters' economic placement and their marriage-ability in adulthood.

INFLUENCE OF LINEAGE ON CHILD DOMESTIC SERVITUDE: STATISTICAL CONTEXT

Patterns of lineage further influence domestic servitude and child labor in other ways. Using findings from the quantitative data, I discuss the relationship between lineage and child labor in the following paragraphs. Prior to that, this subsection discusses patterns of relationships observed between lineage and domestic servitude in the qualitative data.

There were more domestic servants from matrilineal than patrilineal backgrounds in the qualitative research. Out of the 44 current domestic servants who participated in this research, 33 came from matrilineal ethnic backgrounds while the other 11 respondents were patrilineal. Only one former domestic servant was patrilineal. I was not able to interview many former domestic servants from patrilineal backgrounds because I did not visit predominantly patrilineal societies.

I observed that unlike children from matrilineal groups, those from patriliny are more independent of their families whilst they live in servitude and that employers prefer them, especially those from the Northern, Upper East and Upper West Regions, to all other domestic servants. I learned from some employers that they were more humble and hardworking. In this research, all those children who could not trace their parents' houses were members of patrilineal ethnic groups. Furthermore, they lived with total strangers, unlike children from matrilineal backgrounds.

Given their independence of their families while in servitude, I noticed from the qualitative data that domestic servants from patrilineal ethnic groups usually stay longer than those from matrilineal backgrounds. Some of them refuse to return home when they leave their employers' households, choosing instead to independently look for other households in which to live. One employer, for example, told me that she met her previous domestic servant, a northerner, at the market where the latter worked as a porter. It was this porter who asked my respondent to employ her as a domestic servant.

Data from Ghana Statistical Service[7] suggest that the incidence of poverty in patrilineal ethnic groups is higher than it occurs among matrilineal groups. The poverty map on page 31 illustrates this. Domestic servants from such communities, therefore, probably stay longer because of the fear of living in severe poverty should they return to their villages without having become economically independent. It also explains their independence from their families. The current domestic servant of the employer whom I just referenced told me that she and a friend of hers, both 13 at the time, decided to leave school one day and run away to the south to look for jobs as porters or domestic servants.

These observations are corroborated by the statistical analyses of the relationship between lineage and child domestic servitude. Based on the above conclusions, I hypothesized that a relationship existed between lineage and child labor in Ghana and conducted various statistical tests to answer the research question, namely, *what is the role of lineage in the incidence of child labor exploitation in Ghana?* The independent variable in this question is lineage while child domestic labor is the dependent variable.

Table 5.1 provides the frequency distribution of ethnic groups among the participants in the survey. The variable of lineage was derived from these ethnic groups, bearing in mind that of all the groups covered in the survey and in fact in the whole of Ghana only Akans are matrilineal. The survey covers more ethnic groups than did the interviews. The qualitative research contained responses from Ewes, Akans, Gas, and Kusasi. When ethnicity is transformed into lineage with the two response variables of "patriliny" and "matriliny" while the "other" category is excluded in addition to all missing cases, the outcome is presented in Table 5.2. I treated the "other" category as missing because of the fact that in reality there is no additional category of lineage among the research population. Table 3.3 shows that 45% of the sample is matrilineal while the other 55% is patrilineal.

Table 5.1: Distribution of Ethnic Groups

	Frequency	Percentage
Akan	7,387	44.3
Ga-Adangbe	1,240	7.4
Ewe	1,953	11.7
Guan	621	3.7
Gurma	1,200	7.2
Mole-Dagbani	3,111	18.7
Grussi	590	3.5
Mande	318	1.9
Other	237	1.4
Total	**16,657**	**100.0**

Table 5.2: Distribution of Lineage

	Frequency	Percentage
Matrilineal	7,387	45.0
Patrilineal	9,033	55.0
Total	16,420	100.0

Both the dependent (child labor) and the independent (lineage) variables of the research question above were categorical, hence the following numerous chi-square tests were conducted to determine if bivariate associations exist between the independent variable and the dependent variables, the level of strength of the association between them, if any, and the pattern or direction of that association. Child labor is operationalized as "child workers" or "child servants" using the new variables created earlier. However, given the broad nature of "child labor" as a dependent variable, other variables were selected to make the tests focused. These dependent variables were relationship with the head of household (whether good or bad), educational attainment, reasons for working, expectations of what would happen if respondents stopped working, respondents' future goals, and their relationship to their household heads.

Hypothesis Test 1: Relationship between Lineage and the incidence of Child Domestic Servitude

H_0 = no association exists between lineage and child servants;

H_1 = an association exists between lineage and child servants.

Table 5.3: Relationship between Incidence of Child Domestic Servitude and Lineage

Status of Enrollment	Matrilineal No.	Matrilineal %	Patrilineal No.	Patrilineal %	Total No.	Total %
Other Relatives	580	81.7	631	85.9	1,211	83.8
Non-relatives	130	18.3	104	14.1	234	16.2
Total	710	100.0	735	100.0	1,445	100.0

Pearson chi-square (X^2) = 4.6   DF = 1   Sig. P = .032   Phi = -.056

The hypothesis above was tested through a two-way contingency table analysis. The main goal was to determine if lineage influences the decision about whom the domestic servants live with—relatives or non-relatives. The variables were lineage with two nominal levels, namely patriliny and matriliny, and child servants, also with two nominal levels, namely other relatives and non-relatives of respondents' household heads. Table 5.3 provides the results of these analyses.

Nearly 82% of respondents coming from matrilineal backgrounds live with other relatives while a little over 18% of them live with non-relatives. Among patrilineal groups approximately 86% live with relatives while close to 14% live with non-relatives. In that table, we observe this relationship to be statistically significant at α = .05 [Pearson chi-square (X^2) = (1, N=1,445) = 4.61, sig. = .032]. The null hypothesis of no association between lineage and child servants was thus rejected. The phi ($\emptyset$ = -.056) indicates, however, that this association is only moderate, thus confirming the earlier observation made in the qualitative analyses. While this test shows that a moderate relationship exists between lineage and child domestic servitude, it is observed that children from both patrilineal and matrilineal households are more likely to live with other relatives than non-relatives. This similarity notwithstanding, it is further observed that children from patrilineal ethnic groups are more likely to live with relatives than non-relatives, and children from matrilineal ethnic groups are more likely to live with non-relatives.

As shown earlier, the qualitative analyses corroborate existing findings that poverty is the primary cause of child labor exploitation. Among participants in the qualitative part of this research, escaping rural poverty either before or after completing or dropping out of elementary school dominates the reasons for children's acceptance of employment into domestic servitude. In Hypothesis Test 2, this research aimed at finding out if a statistical association exists between lineage and child domestic servitude.

Hypothesis Test 2: Association between Lineage and Reasons for Children's Work

H_0 = no association exists between lineage and reasons why children work;

H_1 = an association exists between lineage and reasons why children work.

Table 6.1 presents the findings from a two-way contingency test conducted to determine if any statistical association exists between these two variables. Unlike Hypothesis Test 1, which included only children living with other relatives and non-relatives, Hypothesis Test 2 included all children, namely those who live with their parents, sons/daughters-in-law, grandchildren, and brothers and sisters who were aged below 18 years. Sons- and daughters-in-law were included in this test primarily because of their age and because they are not heads of their households or the spouses of the household head. Their age and relationship to the household head, it was presumed, make them dependents of their fathers and/or mothers-in-law who headed their households.

Given a Pearson chi-square (X^2) (7, N = 6,204) = 136, sig. = .000 and α = .05, data again confirm the relationship between lineage and child labor. Consequently, the H_0 of no association between lineage and reasons why people work is rejected. A Cramer's V score of .15, nevertheless, is an indication that this relationship is not a strong one.

From the table, we observe that less than .5% of patrilineal and matrilineal children work in Ghana to settle their families' outstanding debts. A majority of them (nearly 51% of matrilineal children and 64.2% of patrilineal children) work in order to supplement their household incomes. Closely related to the quest of supplementing household income is children's need to work to support household enterprises. As much as 41% of matrilineal and 29% of patrilineal children work to help household enterprises. Although the inability to afford school fees should be related to the need for children to work to support their family business or to supplement household incomes, only 2% of matrilineal and 2.3% of patrilineal children work because they cannot afford school fees. These small proportions of those who work because of inability to pay tuition corroborates the observation in the interviews that a large number of the participants had been able to complete the basic education but needed support for further training or schooling. This could also mean that the Free Compulsory Universal Basic Education (FCUBE), which is discussed in detail in Chapter Seven, has been successful at ensuring that children go to school without any financial costs to their parents or guardians.

Given the main focus of this study on children who usually leave their own families to work for other households as resident servants, the above test was re-conducted, but relationship to the head of household was recoded and controlled. As stated earlier, relationship to head of households was recoded first to include the heads' children and grandchildren but excluding siblings, in-laws, and spouses. When we control for relationship to the head of household, we observe a slight change in the proportions of children who work to either support their family incomes or to help family enterprises.

Nearly 51% of matrilineal and 64% of patrilineal children who live with "other relatives" work to support their households' income. Among those who live with non-relatives, 36% of matrilineal and 48% of patrilineal children work to supplement household incomes. The data also shows that about 30% of matrilineal and 29.7% of children who live with other relatives work to support family enterprises. Furthermore, nearly 29% of matrilineal and 40% of patrilineal children who live with "other relatives" work to support family enterprises.

Table 6.1: Bivariate Association between Reasons why Children Work and Lineage

Reasons for Working	Matrilineal No.	%	Patrilineal No.	%	Total No.	%
To supplement household Income	1,145	50.8	2,537	64.2	3,682	59.3
To pay outstanding household Debt	2	.1	4	.1	6	.1
To help in household enterprise	933	41.4	1,162	29.4	2,095	33.8
Education or training program not useful	3	.1	9	.2	12	.2
Education or training institution too far	2	.1	24	.6	26	.4
Cannot Afford School or training fees	44	2.0	90	2.3	134	2.2
Child not interested in school	53	2.4	50	1.3	103	1.7
Other	72	3.2	74	1.9	146	2.4
Total	**2,254**	**100.0**	**3,950**	**100.0**	**6,204**	**100.0**

Pearson chi-square $(X^2) = 136$ DF = 7   Sig. P = .000
Cramer's V = .148

When we include the control variable of "child servants," the data does not provide enough evidence against the H_0 of no association between lineage and children who live with other relatives, given a Pearson chi-square (X^2) (5, N= 434) = 5.45 and a Cramer's V score of .363. We therefore fail to reject the null hypothesis in relation to child servants who live with other family members. For children who live with non-relatives, however, a statistically significant relationship exists between lineage and child servants, given Pearson chi-square (X^2) (4, N = 128) = 10.54 and α = .05. A Cramer's V of .032 indicates though that this relationship is only moderate.

OTHER TRADITIONAL PRACTICES AND CHILD DOMESTIC SERVITUDE

Besides gender and lineage, other cultural practices such as traditional beliefs about infant mortality also played a role in the incidence of domestic servitude, although this was particularly characteristic of the older cohorts of former domestic servants. The reasons for the enrollment of the domestic servants who lived circa 1960s were more cultural than economic. This subsection discusses these other cultural reasons that allow children to live with other families.

Yvonne is one of the older cohorts of the former domestic servants. I met her at Nankasido, a village near Saltpond where I interviewed Lydia's—a current domestic servant—relative and recruiter. Yvonne was sent to live with her father's aunt when she was "very, very young, I had just started walking when they came for me," she said. She could not explain the purpose of her stay with her father's relation because "in those days, mothers allowed their children to live with their fathers' relations. Therefore we the children cannot explain why our mothers sent us away...." Yvonne started school while living with her father's relative but dropped out when she went back to her parents. Her mother came for her when her aunt beat her for losing an earring. At her mother's place, she went back to school but dropped out because she was a "spoilt kid," she concluded. She could do whatever she liked because her parents did not want to upset her.

Religious beliefs also characterized the older generation's stay with other families, hence the cultural influence on domestic servitude in those days. According to oral history, when a woman experienced a high rate of childbirth, it was believed that the same child kept reincarnating. Part of the belief was that such a child had another mother in the spirit world, a mother who needed to be pacified in order to guarantee the earthly survival of the child. Yvonne and Tanya, another respondent from the same village and same era of domestic servitude, survived the constant child mortality that their mothers experienced. Therefore, although they did not categorically indicate that their parents decided to give them away in order to subvert their risk of early mortality, I suspected this was a possible reason; both indicated that in those days, children had to live with their father's sisters, this explaining why they were sent away at early ages. They could not, however, explain why children had to live with their paternal aunts although that negated the Akan's tradition of matriliny. Coming from matrilineal families, both Yvonne and Tanya should have been given to their mothers' relatives. Their stay with paternal relatives explains more the theory that they had to be sent outside the family.

Another instance where cultural practices play a role in domestic servitude is the influence of godparents in the lives of their godchildren. It is traditional, and honorary, for Ghanaians to name their children after family and non-family members. Often, parents would name their children after people in appreciation of their favorable influence at some time in their lives. Children are also named after people in the belief that the child would grow up to follow in the steps of their godparents in terms of economic successes, respectability, and good behavior. Therefore, when naming their children, parents usually choose to name them after admirable and successful people.

Others name their children after relatives or friends out of love. Such is the case of Patricia whose parents named her after her father's half-sister. At age 10, her aunt, the person for whom she was named, came for her to help her go through formal education. Patricia's mother suggested that they allow her to stay with her aunt out of the love her husband had for her, rather than the possibility of not being able to take care of their daughter. Unfortunately, this aunt sent Patricia to her daughter in Accra who needed a maidservant to perform household chores and babysit. Patricia did go to school, through the J.S.S., but her cousin failed to fulfill the aunt's initial promise of sending her to a good private school. Rather than being made to feel a part of the family, she remained an outsider throughout the nine years that she stayed with her cousin and was allowed very limited access to the family's resources. She was also subjected to physical abuse. Her cousin and employer slapped her on the cheeks and would, at the least provocation, hit her with any convenient object. At the time of her exit from this servitude, she had an ear infection that had resulted from the beatings. When she completed the J.S.S., she had hopes of going to work as an apprentice in a hairdressing salon, but her employer failed to pay the fees. Instead, she had to work in this employer's bakery without pay.

CHAPTER SUMMARY AND CONCLUSION

We observe from above that culture plays an enormous role in children's enrollment into domestic servitude. Some of the reasons for the children's willingness to accept offers of domestic servitude point to this conclusion. The dominance of girls in domestic servitude stems from the notion that domestic or household responsibilities are feminine and, therefore, the work of women and girls. This is a cultural expectation. Some parents, employers, and domestic servants told me that the duties of domestic servants are feminine and thus the domain of women or girls. Another aspect of this notion is the domestic servants' hope of learning these feminine skills which, according to them, will make them good wives.

The girls' expectation of becoming financially able to learn hairdressing or dressmaking is another indicator of the role of culture in child domestic servitude. In Ghana, these two occupations are perceived to be feminine. There are many male dressmakers; however, Ghanaians usually use the term of "dressmakers" to refer to women who earn their living by sewing, while referring to males in the same occupation as "tailors." In addition to that distinction, the Ghanaian tailor usually specializes in male clothing while the female concentrates on clothes for women. This observation may not hold true for fashion designers who acquired their training from advanced training institutions such as polytechnics.

Finally and most importantly, I observed that this type of child labor emerged from an existing practice that ensured that children could live with older members of their extended families and be provided with skill training as well as formal education. This quest of economic independence for their young family members lingers today. Nevertheless, this relationship is no longer limited to adults and children who come from the same extended families. The pursuit of economic gains, especially on the part of the employing households, is an exploitation of this historical practice.

Chapter VI

CHILD DOMESTIC SERVITUDE AS A HOUSEHOLD SURVIVAL STRATEGY

As indicated in Chapter Five, child domestic servitude exists in Ghana today because its consumers have exploited a long-standing tradition that evolved out of patterns of extended family relationships. Gradually, newly married women or mothers requested the services of non-family members with the promise of supporting them financially through education or skill training. In recent times when Ghana's economy became deteriorated following political instability and the onset of unsuccessful neo-liberal economic policies, the need for children as domestic servants took a new turn. While the demand for children to baby-sit or to keep the house in order for a mother to work professionally did not decline; patrons of domestic servants needed them for the added responsibilities of keeping shops or selling foodstuffs. This corroborates the theory of the multiple modes of livelihood discussed in Chapter One.

In the following subsections I present observations about child domestic servitude as a means of survival strategy and outline benefits of domestic servitude to employers, domestic servants, and their families. Although the families of child domestic servants benefit from the work of their young members, this study does not support the theory that the survival of such families depends on the children's work. Rather, I argue that employers are the primary, and in some cases, the sole beneficiaries of child domestic servitude. The long hours of work performed by domestic servants and the lack of remuneration for some of them explain this assertion. In this chapter I also discuss the domestic servants' responsibilities.

ECONOMIC BENEFITS THAT ACCRUE TO EMPLOYERS OF DOMESTIC SERVANTS

The practice of child domestic servitude in Ghana is economically beneficial to employers, and to some extent, to the servants' family. Neo-liberal economic policies worsened the existing poor living conditions in rural Ghana. Nevertheless, as the theory of multiple modes of livelihood suggests (Owusu, 2001), these policies impoverished urban households as well (Owusu, 2001). Consequently, both rural and urban residents have had to diversify their means of survival to cope with worsened living conditions. Domestic servants help employing households to generate incomes through petty trading or by taking on the responsibility of household chores while the female heads engage in full time employment outside the home. As for the domestic servants' families, their benefits derive from the reduction in household dependency ratios once their daughters leave home to work as domestic servants. In this section, I present the employing household's benefits derived from child domestic servitude.

Domestic servants are usually assigned three broad responsibilities. These are exclusive household and babysitting chores, exclusive retailing responsibilities, and a combination of both. According to my observations, the type or combination of tasks performed by domestic servants depends on where they live and work. As I explain below, instances occur where employers in both urban and semi-urban communities live with two or more domestic servants in order that there will be a constant supply of free labor for their petty trading. Although children live with other families in rural areas, my limited observations during this research indicate that it is very rare for them to be treated as domestic servants. Typically they go to school and share household responsibilities with their hosts' children. They rarely suffer the out-group positions that characterize domestic servants in urban regions. As out-group members of the households in which they work, some domestic servants eat different foods, are not permitted to play like other children their age within the household nor enjoy household entertainment facilities such as the television, stereos, and games.

I observed from the qualitative data that urban or semi-urban employers who assign their servants both household and commercial responsibilities fit the principles of the multiple models of livelihood model. Commercial responsibilities and household chores in which domestic servants are engaged make it possible or easy for their employers to diversify their sources of income or to save the monies that would have been paid adult domestics for the same duties. Enyonam, for instance, first lived with and sold pastries for a teacher at Ho in the Volta Region (refer to map on page 30). The husband of her current employer, a school teacher, was bedridden with stroke at Accra. Thus, while she kept a shop for this family, she also took care of the sick man and assisted with other household chores.

Another employer relying on multiple modes of survival was a Kumasi-based secondary school teacher who lived with Serwah and Afriyie. When I interviewed her, she indicated that she has domestic servants so they could sell bagged water for her. Afriyie was the first servant and sold at least C50,000 worth of water a day. She was 16 at the time of the interview and had been living with the current employer for five years. She dropped out of school before her recruitment. The employer had three young children; the oldest of them was six at the time of the interview, the youngest was a year old. She decided to go for a second helper who would concentrate on the sale of bagged water to students while Afriyie did strictly household chores. She was, however, disappointed with Serwah's performance and so decided to switch their responsibilities—Serwah to carry out household chores while Afriyie sold the water. At Cape Coast, Mavis made and sold pastries for her employer while the latter worked as a full-time teacher.

In semi-urban communities domestic servants mostly work at their employers shops or sell their wares or foods around town. At Tikobo #1 in the Western Region, I interviewed four servants, two of whom kept shops while the others hawked some type of homemade ice-lolly. Hawa, Ahmed's niece and recruit mentioned in previous chapters, was one of them. Like Serwah and Afriyie's employer, this employer had two servants. The second servant was 16 years of age when I interviewed her employer. She was eight at the time of recruitment. Hawa's employer had given birth and realized she needed another hand if she were to maintain her business. So Hawa was recruited purposely for the business while the older servant continued working around the house and on the employer's farm.

Even when households do not require domestic servants for commercial purposes, they derive net financial benefits from them. As I indicated earlier, the domestic servant's presence in the household makes it possible for the mother in said household to take full-time employment. A large number of the current domestic servants interviewed in urban centers took care of children and performed other household duties such as cleaning, cooking, doing the laundry, and going to the market or shops while the female heads went to work. Ordinarily, households can employ a paid adult to perform these duties professionally. With the exception of domestic servants recruited through formal agencies, all the others are either underpaid or never paid at all for taking care of children, doing general household chores or for trading for the employing household.

Domestic servants in this research work 10 to 18 hours a day. Some of them work longer than that. They usually wake up before six a.m. Almost all of them sweep and dust as first chores. They take a break to prepare breakfast for the family and to get the children, if any, ready to go to school. The fortunate ones will then take a break till noon when they prepare lunch for the children. Otherwise, they continue with their chores. When everybody is gone, they clean the bathrooms, do the laundry, go to the market, and return to prepare lunch and dinner. By the time they go to bed, it will be long past 10 p.m.

Since age nine when she became a domestic servant, Samira for instance, awakened around five a.m. every day. She first cleaned the house if it was her household's turn to do so and then went hawking. She helped to cook on her return from school and then went back to her commercial activities. In the mornings, she sold rice, sugar or pastries. In the evenings, she kept a shop after cooking. In addition to ordinary grocery items like seasoning and canned foods, she sold alcoholic beverages and cigarettes, even at age nine.

Patricia, who lived with her godmother's daughter while going to school, helped with her relative's bread-making business in addition to other household chores. When she completed the J.S.S., her cousin's promise of enrolling her in a hairdressing apprenticeship was never fulfilled because of the free services she provided in the bakery. I asked her if the experience there was not enough to make her a baker. She explained that she could not bake because she was only allowed to run errands or help knead the dough; she was not allowed to learn about the ingredients added to the flour or the detailed processes of making the bread. At a very young age, Molly, who went to live with her late father's friend and his family at age four, had to clean and light the lamps in her benefactor's guesthouse where they also stayed. She said some of the guests liked her and so gave her tips.

Payment for Domestic Services

From the above we observe that children sometimes receive skill training through their responsibilities as domestic servants. Although this research does not condone child labor exploitation, it discovers that the trading and other responsibilities are skills that, when learned, can help the servants to become economically independent during adulthood. Using ILO's definition, the potential for children to learn skills from these responsibilities make it easy to refer to them as performing positive children's work. Besides ILO's categorization of children's employment into positive and negative children's work as outlined in Chapter Two, it argues that

> Children work because their survival and that of their families depend on it, and in many cases, because unscrupulous adults take advantage of their vulnerability. It is also due to inadequacies and weaknesses in national education systems. It is deeply ingrained in cultural and social attitudes and traditions (ILO C182: 11).

Contrary to this assertion, survival of the giving-families in this research is not dependent on their children's deployment into domestic servitude. By this assertion I do not imply that the families of domestic servants do not in any way benefit from their children's work. Rather, I acknowledge the fact that the benefits accruing to them relative to those enjoyed by the children's employers tends to be infinitesimal, especially given the fact that some domestic servants do not get paid at all. Families of domestic servants enjoy the indirect benefits of being spared the burden of taking care of their young members when they live in and work for other households. In the past, families had the additional privilege of saving the cost of puberty rites when their children's employers took up the responsibility to organize and sponsor this initiation ceremony.

According to the data, child domestic servants do not usually have any income to give to their families. We learned in Chapter Four that where there is a non-formal recruiter involved, the family's chances of seeing their child's income when a contract is curtailed is even minimal. The reason is that their recruiters, as Chapter Four suggests, save the money for them while they reassign them to new households. Only a few of those who arrange to receive monthly incomes can think of sending monies to their families, but that is rare.

For working 10 to 18 hours a day providing the services I outlined above, the highest paid among the non-formally or informally recruited current domestic servants received C90,000 (approximately $9.50) a month at the time of this research. Among those recruited through formal agencies, the minimum pay was C150,000. Other employers in the non-formal and informal categories of recruitment choose to pay their servants off at the end of their service. The usual means of payment when payment is deferred towards end of their contracts, as indicated earlier, is an enrollment in an apprenticeship, either to become a hairdresser or a seamstress.

Employers justify their underpayment of domestic servants with the claim of taking care of their basic needs and medical expenses. In Akosua's statement cited (on page 38), her employers promised to pay her C80,000 a month besides her living expenses. Akosua's employers kept her salaries for her, but she could always request part of it for her personal effects, usually clothing. Others employer that I interviewed also emphasized their daily expenses for their servants.

At the time of recruitment employers usually arrange with families or the servants themselves the method of payment and how much it should be. On average, employers agree to enroll them in the apprenticeship after two years of service. Depending on the location and the background of the trainer, the entry fees can range between C200.000 and C1 million (i.e. between $22.00 and 120.00). In the case of domestic servants who choose to become dressmakers, employers must also provide sewing machines and the necessary tools to start the training. Domestic servants who opt for hairdressing may receive hairdryers; otherwise they may buy them on their own when they complete their training and become independent.

Employers who agree to pay a monthly wage usually give the correct amount should the domestic servant decide to leave at any time. Derrick's and Sophia's recruits, who were discussed earlier, received the exact amount due them when they chose to curtail their employment, albeit underpayment.

In this research only one of the participants, Akosua, who lived with a university faculty member, ever sent part of her pay to her mother. After living with her employers for seven months, she collected four months' pay and sent an equivalent of one month's pay, i.e. C80,000 (about $9.50) to her mother who was then taking care of her two-year-old son. This kind of gesture did not occur often among my respondents. Even those who stay long enough to be enrolled in an apprenticeship hardly have anything to contribute to their families back home. When domestic servants curtail their service before apprenticeship, they stand a chance of returning home with some money and clothing or a sewing machine. On rare occasions do families usurp such resources without saving them for the domestic servants.

Current domestic servants who had lived with other families before told me that their parents saved their previous remuneration, which was always meager, as a supplement for their future skill training. When I met Enyonam, she was living with her third employer. Both previous employers gave her a sewing machine, each when she was leaving. She was lucky in that throughout her previous servitudes she had remained in school until she completed the J.S.S. When I asked her what she did with the two machines, she told me her mother was keeping them for her. Later she said they were looking for somebody to sell one to, but she was not sure how much it would sell for.

Indisputably, families enjoy the benefit of not feeding or bearing the living expenses of another household member once they are recruited into domestic servitude. The hope of the child coming home with money and equipment to start learning a trade is also comforting. This hope is almost universal in the respondents. Some of them had lost both parents and had no caretaker. Angela went into domestic servitude for the reason that both of her parents were deceased. As stated above, her uncle who succeeded her father had his own children to care for. As a minimum-wage earner, he could not adopt and fend for his brother's ten orphaned children. Consequently, he looked for an employer for her. When she had to be recruited the second time but did not want to accept the offer following her bitter experience with her former employer, her uncle successfully persuaded her, under the circumstances of financial constraint, to rescind her decision.

What I heard most in those interviews included "my parents could not further my education"; "I had no one to take care of me"; "my mother could no longer finance my education"; and "I am in poverty," and other similar statements. Given these reasons, once recruited into domestic servitude, parents, guardians, and/or the extended family members responsible for the upkeep of the children are relieved.

At times, generous employers send remittances to their domestic servants' parents. As stated in Chapter Four, Kate's employer gave a certain amount of money to Derrick for her mother. Gloria's employer indicated that she gave old clothing to her father when he visited them once. Gloria recalled that her employer gave some money to her father but she was not sure how much it was. Other generous employers saw their servants' off in a manner that would invariably benefit their families. Mrs. Biney told me that at one time she performed the puberty rites of her domestic servant, saving the family the cost and drudgery of sponsoring it themselves. As she described it, "we bought so many things and gave them away,

cloths, towels, shoes and cosmetics, and...a lot of things. Powder, they specified the quantity to buy." At the time of the interview, Hawa's employer, who
was preparing to send her 16 year-old-servant away, told me, "At the moment,
I have one who might be going away at the end of the month. She is old. I have
therefore been making the preparations so that when she gets home, her mother
would realize that her child lived with a good person." She did not specify what
she was giving to this servant but did confirm it would include a sewing machine,
clothing, and money.

Given devout adherence to cultural practices such as initiation ceremonies
in the years before the 1980s, remuneration for the older generation of domestic
servants in this research took the form of puberty rites sponsorship. These older
women specified that girls who lived with relatives before the 1970s and 1980s
did not expect any form of remuneration for their services even when they were
not enrolled in formal education. The only exception was Esther who shared a lot
in common with post-1980 domestic servants and had to live with three employers
and usually agreed with them on the method of payment before her recruitment.

Many are those who run away without informing their employers and forfeit
all their entitlements. There are instances where employers refuse to give any
gifts or payment package to their outgoing servants even when they have over-
stayed the usual two years, if the employers think they are leaving on a bitter note.
Samira and Patricia, two former domestic servants who experienced this situation,
lived with two relatives. As discussed earlier, Patricia lived with her first cousin.
She was only 10 years of age when her father's sister, after whom she was named,
came for her with the intention of having Patricia live with her daughter, Patricia's
cousin. At the time of this interview, Patricia was 20 years of age and had returned
to her parents. This servant's employer, her cousin, refused to fulfill her promise
of sending her through hairdressing apprenticeship because the servant's mother
had paid them a visit, the first in nine years. On her part, Samira lived with her
mother's stepmother for four years. When her mother decided to come for her,
her step-grandmother's daughter was highly upset and so advised her mother, the
'employer,' to take everything from the girl. She went back home with nothing.

More often than not, employers never fulfilled their part of the agreement to
send off domestic servants after two to three years. Contrary to the usually agreed
period of two years, it took at least four years for employers to enroll their servants
in any type of apprenticeship; Hawa's employer lived with her other servant, the 16-
year-old, for a period of eight years before thinking of buying her the machine and
other tools to send her off. Afriyie lived with her employer for close to five years
before being enrolled in an apprenticeship. Soon after her enrollment her employer
advised that she quit because of reports that the trainer did not show up regularly.
Afriyie's employer promised to re-enroll her at a different place, but that can take
a while. Another respondent at Nungua, a suburb of Accra, started a hairdressing
apprenticeship after six years of service. Her employers did not have to pay the
usual fees because the trainer is related to them. That notwithstanding, the servant

had to stop the training at the request of her employers, their reason being that the hairdressing salon was too far from home. They promised to look for another trainer closer to their house for her, but after six months, this respondent had still not heard them mention anything about enrolling her in a training program.

While these employers could have good intentions in stopping their servants from going to work, there could be other motives. For instance, hairdressing and dressmaking apprentices are as much exploited by their trainers as by the employers with whom they live. Apprentices perform many chores for their bosses, some of which are unrelated to their training (Marguerat, 2000) and, therefore, they have to be at work very early in the mornings and sometimes leave late at night. Most of them go to work six days a week. Hairdressing and dressmaking apprentices in Ghana help their trainers in the provision of services to their clients. They have to do these things, without any remuneration, as part of their training. In the rural areas some apprentices perform household chores and go to the farms for their trainers. The implication of this is the unavailability of the servant to provide free domestic services for her employer. Hence, the real motive behind their withdrawal could be the retention of lost hours of free services rather than distance or trainer's absenteeism.

As already indicated, domestic servants, other than those recruited through the formal agencies, were either underpaid or never paid at all. Worst of all is the experience of those who curtail their contracts and lose everything due them. In conclusion, that families give their children into domestic servitude in order that such families would survive is a myth, at least for the participants in this study. Most of them are not paid, and when they are, their employers or recruiters hold the money for them. Interviews with the servants, their parents, recruiters, and employers confirm that families receive very little if anything from their children's servitude. Employers, on the other hand, use domestic servants to cut costs or to generate incomes to supplement their household's resources. Therefore if there are any economic benefits from domestic servitude, the sole beneficiaries are the employers. Until children serve longer than the agreed period or live with numerous employers, they might not be able to start learning any skills unless their parents provide the resources for it.

How Child Workers Are Paid: Statistical Evidence

The qualitative analyses concluded that domestic servants are paid in cash at the end of the month if they were recruited through formal or non-formal agencies or mostly at the end of their service, usually in kind. Although the survey asked questions about how child workers are remunerated and who the beneficiaries are, the findings do not indicate that many of the respondents were paid for their services. According to the data, only 1.5% of the 17,034 participants get paid for their services. As much as 98.5% do not get paid at all. Analyses of bivariate association between child domestic servitude (defined by relationship to the head of household and having response variables "not related" and "other relatives") and how they are remunerated evidenced a somewhat strong relationship between these two variables, given a Cramer's V score of .553. A Pearson chi-square (X^2) (4, N = 60) of 18.35 (.001) also reveals a statistically significant relationship between child domestic servitude and how they are paid.

Table 6.2: Bivariate Association between Method of Remuneration and Relationship to Head of Household

Method of Pay	Relative		Other Relatives		Total	
	No.	%	No.	%	No.	%
Piece Rate	11	30.6	2	8.3	13	21.7
Daily	9	25.0	2	8.3	11	18.3
Weekly	4	11.1	0	0	4	6.7
Monthly	5	13.9	15	62.5	20	33.3
5 Yearly	7	19.4	5	20.8	12	20.0
Total	**36**	**100.0**	**24**	**100.0**	**60**	**100.0**

Pearson chi-square (X^2) = 18.35   DF = 4   Sig. P = .001
Cramer's V = .553

Findings, presented in Table 6.2 corroborate observations in the qualitative analyses that domestic servants are not regularly compensated for their services. Only 60 (4%) of the 1,445 who were defined as domestic servants were paid. Of those 60 domestic servants, 60% live with other relatives while the other 40% live with non-relatives. The implication of this is that domestic servants who live with their relatives are more likely to be compensated for the services they provide.

We observe further in that table that nearly 30% of those who live with other relatives and a little over 8% of those who live with non-relatives are remunerated on a piece rate basis. Additionally, a third (33.3%) of domestic servants is paid regularly on a monthly basis, while 20% is paid after five years. Of all those who live with non-relatives, 62% (i.e. 75% of those who are paid on a monthly basis) are paid regularly on a monthly basis. The statistical data does not provide any information on how respondents are recruited; therefore, very little inference could be made and related to conclusions made from the qualitative analyses. Conclusions that respondents who are recruited through formal and non-formal agencies are more likely to be paid regularly at the end of the month cannot be replicated with all certainty at this stage of the analyses because of the lack of information on how participants in the survey were recruited.

WHY DOMESTIC SERVANTS PREMATURELY LEAVE SERVITUDE

I suggested earlier that domestic servants who did not stay until employers decided to enroll them into the training of choice usually stood the risk of not receiving payment for their services. This observation notwithstanding, some domestic servants preferred to leave, at times without informing their employers and thus losing their benefits. Out of the 44 current domestic servants in this research, 19 had lived with more than one family. Seven of the former domestic servants of the post-1980 era lived with at least two households before settling down. Given that some respondents knew they stood the risk of losing their accrued incomes or the chance of being enrolled into an apprentice training should they leave on their own, I asked questions about what drove them to take such risks. Using the microeconomic theory of utility maximization, I concluded that until domestic servants and their families realize their goals for being a part of domestic servitude, young women and children will continue to reenroll as servants. This subsection describes conditions that prompt domestic servants to desert their work.

While disparate experiences and reasons contribute to their exit from any household, the domestic servants' or their parents' hope of the former accumulating adequate incomes or sufficiently pleasing their employers so as to find the means to learn a type of trade was very common. It was so rare for any other respondent, current or past, apart from Lily (see Chapter Eight on slavery), or even their parents, to categorically state that they needed to be in servitude; otherwise their families could not feed them. I observed that they derive their spirit of persistence in servitude from this hope of future economic independence rather than from current gratitude from basic necessities such as food, clothing and shelter. Families are more concerned about their offspring's future independence rather than incomes to be acquired through exploitation of the latter's labor. Given this background, one might wonder why girls would leave domestic servitude when the goals are yet to be realized. The rest of this subsection examines the causes of premature departure among domestic servants.

Generally, three things drive either the employer or the domestic servant to end the "contract" prematurely. Besides the usual dissatisfaction with the servants work, when employers ask their servants to leave prematurely, it is usually because of the latter's contact with or intentions to visit their families and/or the employers' suspicions of their servants having boyfriends. The servants also leave because their employers' house is quiet, for sexual abuses, or if they are wrongfully accused. I did not meet any respondent who had to leave for long hours of hard work or for non-payment of services. Only one servant disclosed her intentions to leave at the end of the second year if by then she had not been registered to learn a trade. On page 113, I quoted an employer's description of how she sent off a servant who ran away because her new home was so quiet. Emelia's employer also told me that her fourth servant decided to leave because their residence was too quiet for her.

Amina is another servant who ended her agreement with two employers, her reasons being that the first place was too quiet for her , while she left the second servitude, because her employer advised her to after she decided to pay a visit to her parents. I met her in a small village in the Ashanti Region. She had already lived with three families since dropping out of school. Two months after living with the first person in Kumasi, the Ashanti Regional capital, she ran away without informing them. Her reason for leaving was that the place was too quiet for her. She said she was also afraid to be there all by herself. She was not paid for her services. Although the second employer paid her C90,000 a month, her parents thought the priority was her formal education and so sent for her after a couple of months. Amina did not stay long in school and after dropping out the second time went to live with the third family. Her employer agreed to pay her off at the end of two years. Just around the end of her second year, she requested to visit her parents to celebrate the Easter festivities with them. The man's wife suggested that she pack her things and not return. She received half a million cedis (approximately $80.00) for staying with them for two years. Patricia's experience mentioned earlier is similar to this. Her cousin asked her to go away after Patricia's mother paid her a visit, and as I emphasized earlier, it was the first time in nine years that she had visited.

An isolated case of an employer asking a servant to leave without any provocation on either side took place soon after Mrs. Grace Coleman, the erstwhile MP, was indicted. This particular employer was a member of parliament also. According to Helene, the former domestic servant, this employer lived with six domestic servants simultaneously. One day, without anything having changed in the house or any of them offending her, she told them she could no longer live with any of them and so arranged for them to go away. She made Helene return to her grandmother in the company of "a certain woman," Helene explained. Helene, a J.S.S. graduate, went to live with this MP at the age of 16. It had been arranged that after two years this employer would provide her with the sewing machine and some money to enable her learn a trade. The MP did not give her these things when she made arrangements to send her back to her village. In my interview with her grandmother, I learned that they were making plans to contact the MP for the sewing machine and, if possible, some money for the enrollment fees. She stated further that if this plan failed, they would find another alternative to get Helene to start the training; however, living with another household as a domestic servant was out of the question.

Earlier, I made reference to a third person that Derrick had recruited but whom I could not interview. This servant lived in the same household as Michael, another recruit of Derrick's, and James, the cousin of their employer. According to the employer's wife, this servant was being sexually abused like her predecessors, and in a telephone call to Ghana in 2004, I learned that she had run away as a result of a sexual assault. This girl was 15 at the time of the interview. I could not interview her because she was almost always busy whenever I went to visit her. I held brief discussions with this employer's wife whenever I visited to get one of the servants to interview. She was not in favor of her husband recruiting girls to help around the house because they always complained of his sexual harassment and left. As indicated previously, Michael came from the same village as this girl and their recruiter, Derrick. Their employer accused James of having connived with the girl to escape. The former thought his employer was never pleased with anything that he did subsequent to that accusation and so ran away some weeks later. Neither of these domestic servants were remunerated for their services.

This employer is one of two males who were directly involved in the recruitment and responsibilities of their servants. There were two families in which the men arranged for the recruitment of their domestic servants. Usually, the women did that and kept contact with the children. They seemed more responsible for the domestic servants and houseboys than the men were. The other man was the contact for Amina's recruitment. Therefore, she made reference to him as the employer and to the woman as "the man's wife." Usually, I heard "the woman's" husband.

Two other respondents, Doreen and Akesi, also encountered sexual harassment and left their employers as a result. On page 113, Doreen's first experience with an attempted sexual assault was discussed. This man was never successful in his attempts to abuse her sexually, but after discussing it with a neighbor, she realized it was necessary for her to run away before his wife found out and ended her marriage. She escaped in the night, sleeping behind wooden structures until she was able to hail a taxi at dawn to take her to her hometown. Previously she had been raped at age 15 when she lived with her father's female cousin while her mother sojourned in the Ivory Coast. The culprit was her aunt's son who, in addition to the sexual assault, had beaten her. She reported this to her aunt who later found out that she had become pregnant as a result. They took her to the hospital for an abortion and when they returned from the hospital, her aunt beat her again, mercilessly. The boy also beat her again, telling her that she should not have mentioned his name. When her aunt found out that Doreen had reported this abuse to her father, she threw her out of the house in the dark of midnight.

While Doreen might have been right in anticipating that reporting the man's constant harassment to his wife could have jeopardized his marriage, she could have been kicked out in a similar manner as her aunt had done had she reported the attempted abuses. For Akesi did exactly that and was dismissed by her female employer. Akesi lost her businessman father when she was young. Her paternal uncle inherited the business but refused to finance her and her siblings' education, and consequently, she and her sister ended up in servitude. Her first employer's husband lived in another town and visited from time to time. On one such visit, he attempted to rape her. She did not keep this to herself but reported it to her female employer. When the wife confronted her husband, he advised that the girl be sent away because he did not want her serving the household anymore. After this episode, Akesi looked for another employer without consulting any of her family members. Her mother searched for her for some time, and just as she was about to make a report to the police, she received word of her daughter's job in a local restaurant in a village miles away from the Western Region where they come from.

Besides sexual harassment, verbal and physical abuse seemed to run through most of the interviews. Unless the employer respected the servant and understood the circumstances leading to their choice of such jobs, they, to quote Angela, one of the current domestic servants, "... are treated as though..." they "... are not a part of the human race, that you weren't born."

Domestic servants left servitude for many reasons. However, as the above discussions under this subsection point out, servants are more willing to stay than leave because of the hope of being paid for the services rendered. I argue that if girls accept to go into servitude for any particular reason, such as to be able to eventually learn a trade, they are more willing to stay to fulfill that objective before leaving. In the event that they leave for any reason, they are almost always willing to go into servitude again. In the next subsection, I employ the statistical data to analyze the combination of factors that may determine employee satisfaction with their jobs and employers.

Respondents were asked to indicate whether they considered their relationships with their employers to be good or bad. This dependent variable of "relationship with employer" was recoded from an original variable where responses were "good," 'bad," "other," and "don't know" into "good" and "bad". The rest of the variables were defined as missing and thus excluded from the analyses. The findings show that 154 as opposed to 7 respondents were satisfied with their employers. Given the constant nature of the relationship between servants and their employers, no further tests were conducted on the level of respondents' satisfaction with their employers. To some extent, this observation probably corroborates the qualitative data finding that respondents are willing to stay with their employers until they receive pay for their service. On the contrary, this constancy does not support the qualitative data finding that almost every respondent thought they lived under slavery conditions.

CHAPTER SUMMARY AND CONCLUSION

Domestic servitude exists in Ghana because of cultural and economic reasons. Although the practice of children living with other families has existed in Ghana for a long time, one observes that cultural factors explained domestic servitude in the past. Today, economic factors drive families to either send their children to live with other families or to look for children to live with as domestic servants. The giving families' benefit from child domestic servitude was more indirect than direct. Contrary to assertions in the literature, we observe that families benefited from their children's servitude only to the extent that they do not have to feed them or provide the funds for their children to learn some trades. The employing family, on the other hand, derives both direct and indirect benefits from the use of children's labor in their households. The direct benefits result from the use of these children in petty trading, while the indirect benefits accrue from the nonpayment or underpayment of child domestic servants. Although children have to stay longer than agreed upon before being allowed to start learning a trade, those who are patient enough are able to realize this long term goal. Those who are not able to stay long enough to be put through the training return to their parents, are reassigned households, or their parents fund their apprenticeship. To conclude, the only real beneficiaries of domestic servitude are not the children's families or the victims themselves but the employing households.

Chapter VII

RELATIONSHIP BETWEEN FORMAL EDUCATION AND THE INCIDENCE OF CHILD DOMESTIC SERVITUDE

Education is a major path through which a population's children can be protected from labor exploitation and slavery. Education can keep children busy and thus exclude them from any type of employment. While many children are engaged in what Chapter Two identifies as positive children's work, one observes that un-enrolled children of school going age are more vulnerable to exploitation than those in school. I observed from the qualitative data that rural children are more likely to stay out of school than children in urban Ghana and hence are more vulnerable to labor exploitation. Resource availability, parents' occupational and educational backgrounds, and their expected values on education influence children's participation in formal education. If for any of these reasons, or others, children do not access formal education, they become readily available for work and exploitation, sometimes under slavery conditions. This chapter discusses the relationship between formal education and the incidence of child domestic servitude as well as the influence of parental values placed on their children's educational participation.

GHANA'S FORMAL EDUCATIONAL SYSTEM

The 1998 Children's Act defines the Ghanaian child as all persons below the age of 18. The minimum working age is, however, set at 15. Before this age, the law requires that the child remain in school. Children usually begin school at age six. Until 1987 when Ghana launched its Education Reform Program, there was a 17 year pre-university schooling. This reform program reduced the pre-university school to 12 years. Currently, there is a 6-3-3-4 schooling structure in Ghana. Children are required to spend six years in primary school, three years in junior secondary school (J.S.S.), another three years in senior secondary school (S.S.S.) and four years in the university. The first nine years of schooling, that is the primary and junior secondary schooling, make up the mandatory basic education for all children. Article 25 of Ghana's 1992 Constitution stipulates that the basic education shall be free, compulsory, and available to every child.

While this constitutional provision follows from principles of the Convention on the Rights of the Child discussed in Chapter Two, there are concerns about Ghana's development goal and the relationship between it and the quality of its children. Ghana's development goal is to attain a middle income status by the year 2020. Specific goals and strategies have been outlined in the development plan "Ghana Vision 2020." Indisputably, the quality of its children and adults will be instrumental for the attainment of those specific goals. Prominent among them is a set of educational goals which, although an end in themselves, will contribute to the attainment of the other goals of the plan. The educational goal is to "ensure that all citizens, regardless of gender or social status, are functionally literate and numerate, at the minimum" (Ghana Vision 2020). Two programs have been launched towards these objectives, the Girl's Education Unit and the Free Compulsory Universal Basic Education (FCUBE). The FCUBE program covers three broad objectives. These are improvements in the quality of teaching and learning, improvements in management efficiency, and improvements in accessibility of basic educational facilities.

In line with the third objective of the FCUBE, the Ghana Education Service established the Girls' Education Unit in 1997. This unit is responsible for the development of women's social capital. Among other things, this unit aims at increasing enrollment of girls in basic education to equal that of boys, reducing drop-out rates among girls in primary schools from 30% to 10% and 21% to 15% among girls in junior secondary schools, and enhancing an increase in the transition rate of girls from junior to senior secondary schools by 10% by the end of the FCUBE program. In addition to improving their levels of educational attainment, improvement in women and girls' social capital will advance their bargaining power, their self-confidence, and their decision-making power.

In 1998 when these educational objectives were established, 31% of the population who were aged 15 and above could neither read nor write. In the years that followed, Ghana saw slight improvements in its literacy rates. In 2001, for instance, only 27.3% of the population aged 15 or older could neither read nor write. In 2002, there was a further reduction to 26.2%. The declining trend of the nationwide literacy levels are reflected in the following statistics for females. In 1998, 40% of the female population who were least 15 years of age were literate; in 2001, only 35.5% of females aged 15 or older could neither read nor write. This rate fell to 34.1% of the female population aged 15 and over in 2002. A 1998 estimate shows a 56.8% net primary enrollment of the relevant age group. While gross primary enrollment between 1996 and 2002 stood at a higher rate of 80% of all school-going ages (The World Bank, 2004), primary school enrollment for males stood at approximately 84% with a significantly lower level for females at 76%. In 1998, the estimated net secondary (high) school enrollment was 26.1% of the relevant age group.

PARENTAL INFLUENCE IN THE EDUCATION OF THEIR CHILDREN

Although it is the constitutional right of every Ghanaian child to receive at least the basic education, socio-economic conditions facing their parents and certain traditional beliefs, as suggested in Chapters Two, Four, and Five, deny the child that right to education. Parental occupation and economic backgrounds are among other factors that determine children's vulnerability to child domestic servitude in Ghana. For the purpose of this research, I categorize the economic standards of households into three groups. The first category consists of the middle class through the richest members of the research population. Expatriates, state officials, and employees occupying middle through upper level managerial positions in state and private enterprises fall under this topmost category. The second category consists of people occupying lower level managerial positions as well as self-employed men and women who make basically the same levels of income. According to the World Bank, an estimated 60% of Ghana's population lives above poverty line. These constitute the two levels of economic standards conceptualized here. The other 40% are the poor, of which an estimated 60% live in rural regions and comprise the primary source of free labor supply for domestic servitude in urban regions.

With the exception of the only male parent who participated in this study, none of the parents of the domestic servants in this research ever had high income jobs. This father who was on pension at the time of this interview had worked as an electrician in the Electricity Corporation of Ghana. He finished the elementary school and learned to be an electrician through an on-the-job training program. His wife, whose father had to send her into domestic servitude to avoid the misery of living in rural poverty and becoming a fishmonger, had no job when I conducted this interview. Five of the parents and relatives who lived in the coastal areas of Central Region were fishmongers and or petty traders who sold cooked food. All the parents I interviewed in the Ashanti Region were peasant farmers who had never attended school.

As for the other domestic servants whose parents I could not interview, I observed from their responses that they were mostly petty traders and/or farmers. With the exception of three fathers—one a chainsaw operator, another a Pentecostal church pastor, and the third, a local gin brewer—all their fathers were farmers. The women were mostly farmers, a few of them doubled as petty traders in addition to farming. Neither the parents nor their children could estimate their annual, monthly, or weekly incomes. Farming is seasonal in those communities, and between the cocoa and food crop seasons, these families subsist on what little farm produce they grow and are without regular financial incomes. The petty traders deal in foodstuffs and household consumables such as soaps, canned foods, and seasonings. The women from the coastal areas are usually fishmongers.

Rural parents in Ghana usually were either never enrolled in formal education at all or dropped out some time before graduation. In this research, there was only one elementary school graduate among those whom I interviewed. The others were never enrolled at all or dropped out at the primary school level. This partially explains why most of them lived primarily on farming, petty trading, and fishing or fish-mongering. Ghanaian petty traders usually sell foodstuffs, convenience items, stationery, and clothes. Their own educational backgrounds notwithstanding, some of them do appreciate formal education's potential impact on social mobility and insist on their children's full participation. In his biography, Kwame Nkrumah, the first President of Ghana, emphasized that his mother's incessant struggle to encourage his interest in school compelled him to eventually remain in school and further his education. In contemporary Ghana both rural and urban parents strive to get their children interested in formal education. In an effort to convince their children to remain in school, some parents practically drag and cane their children. In this research, seven of my respondents said that their parents at times removed them from servitude so they could go back to school, although they preferred to not be in school because of poor performance or for punishment by teachers.

This observation does not hold for all cultural areas in the research population. For example, among the rural residents of the coastal Central Region, a person's chances of going to school depended more on their parents' occupation. As some teachers told me, school children preferred to go fishing or to trade in fish at the beach rather than be in school. If their fathers were primarily fishermen and owned fishing equipment, first and second male children were more likely to drop out of school to learn this trade in their early childhoods. In this context, it is probable that the parents might not have experienced the positive impacts of formal education in their own lives and so have ascribed very little value to it.

EDUCATIONAL RESOURCE AVAILABILITY
AND ACCESSIBILITY

Like the main factors explaining child labor in general, cultural and economic reasons are also responsible for low levels of formal education for girls and thus for higher levels of the incidence of labor exploitation among them. This interaction between culture and economic factors both at the local and international levels (Bhavnani, Foran and Kurian, 2003; Young, 1984; Goheen, 1991; Mikell, 1997) makes child labor exploitation gender biased. In addition to parental involvement, children's educational chances depend on resource availability as well as the cultural and economic environments of the group in question. To help understand the economic terrain of the research population, I define three types of communities: namely rural, semi-urban, and urban communities. Rural populations are very small, usually below 5,000. For instance, Hwidiem, one of the rural communities where I interviewed some former domestic servants and some parents, has a population of about 400. Semi-urban communities have populations of at least 5,000. Urban centers, usually enormous, tend to be overcrowded, especially in poor shanty towns, with populations of at least 50,000.

Rural communities are the poorest and have very limited, if any, social amenities or infrastructure. They do not have potable or pipe-borne water, health facilities, and in some cases, primary education. One of the rural communities that I visited during this research had a school with only six grades, from primaries one through six. Beyond the sixth grade, students have to walk two miles to attend school in the nearest village. Some of these villages do have locations near tarred or asphalted trunk roads, thus making it easier for their residents to access schools, hospitals, and markets in nearby towns and cities. At times, rural residents have to travel to and from nearby towns on foot. The poorest among them are located in the hinterlands and are joined to other communities by small, untarred laterite roads. Residents of these communities usually do not have their own vehicles but use private commercial vehicles most of which operate once a week. Table 6.3 below, shows as much as 44% of children who were never enrolled in school indicated that their parents could not afford it. Although the data does not provide respondents' reasons for their lack of interest in schooling, the distance, the fact that it might worsen the financial burdens of their families, and the lack of general educational infrastructure could be the reasons.

To make matters worse, rural schools lack basic resources; this makes learning in them more difficult and unpleasant. Rural schools in Ghana have very few teachers if any at all, and some of them are hardly qualified to teach. Recent studies show that 652 schools in Ghana are short of teachers (Berlan, 2004). Furthermore, some of these rural teachers have been observed to cash in on the labor of their pupils (Cabanes, 2000). According to Robert Cabanes (2000), many rural teachers in former African colonies use their pupils' labor by asking them to fetch water or wood for the formers' personal use. The interplay between the lack of resources, the use of pupils' labor by rural teachers, and the need for children to walk miles to nearby villages and towns to attend J.S.S. could prevent children from participating fully in formal education.

Table 6.3: Why Some Respondents Never Attended School

Reasons	Frequency	Percentage
Parents cannot afford	1,264	44.2
School too far	526	18.4
Not interested in school	488	17.1
Family does not allow schooling	142	5.0
Illness/diabled	60	2.1
Both parents not alive	8	.3
Father not alive	37	1.3
Mother not alive	30	1.0
Other	305	10.7
Total	**2,860**	**100.0**

Consequently, they drop out because of poor academic performance. Ten of the domestic servants who participated in the qualitative study said they dropped out of school because they did not do well academically. Rather than walk miles to nearby villages for school, such children preferred living in urban areas with other families than going through the channels of formal education without any expected outcomes. Even among those who finish school in such rural regions, levels of educational achievement are usually low. Research shows that an estimated 60% of children graduating from junior secondary schools in rural Ghana do not acquire basic literacy (Berlan, 2004).

It is not disputable that poverty exists in urban regions of Ghana as well as it does in rural areas. Francis Owusu and the World Bank and other credible reports confirm that standards of living for urban residents in the research population worsened following poor implementation of economic policies. Nevertheless, access to formal education in urban areas tends to be relatively favorable. The use of children in farming or fishing, although prevalent in urban areas, is not as intense as in rural regions. Both parents and children place more emphasis on education than the latter s' involvement in farming or fishing activities.

Additionally, availability of good infrastructure and learning aid in the cities make it easier for children to keep abreast of their school work if they really want to. The implication of this is that urban children, irrespective of their family's socio-economic backgrounds, are less likely to experience labor exploitation or to live in servitude without receiving at least the basic education. Conversely, Accra, the capital of Ghana and all regional capitals such as Cape Coast, Kumasi, and Takoradi are urban communities. These towns have advanced educational institutions such as polytechnics and universities. Unless district capitals had such advanced centers of learning, they were considered semi-urban. The semi-urban communities have characteristics of both the rural and the urban. Most of them have secondary schools and a few other vital institutions such as banks, police stations, and post offices. The most developed amongst them have hospitals and schools affiliated with universities. The poorest among them have no secondary schools but can boast of health posts, which are markedly different from conventional hospitals. Health posts usually do not have medical doctors but medical assistants or nurses. Some of the semi-urban centers are just over-grown communities, encountering higher rates of urbanization without any matching improvements in social amenities. While both the urban and semi-urban communities have most of the amenities and infrastructure (such as telephones, paved roads, post offices, and potable water), necessary to make living conditions bearable, overcrowding and overpopulation negate these advantages for most residents.

Table 6.4 is the mean distribution of school educational participation in the various regions. From that table, we observe that Upper West, Upper East, and Northern Regions (the poorest regions in the country) experience the lowest rates of school participation in Ghana. We notice further that although educational attainment tends to be generally low, children from poor regions are less likely to be enrolled.

A cross-tabulation of regions by educational participation also shows a statistical relationship between these two variables. A Pearson chi-square (X^2) (54, N = 16,967) of 3,037 (.000) is highly significant at α = .05. Nevertheless, a Cramer's V score of .23 shows the strength of this relationship is less than moderate. From Table 6.5, we observe a marked distinction in formal educational participation between Northern, Upper East, and Upper West Regions on one hand, and all other regions on the other. As Map II illustrates, these three Northern Regions—namely Upper East, Upper West and Northern Regions—are the poorest in the country. School participation in Greater Accra Region (where the Capital of Ghana is located) is highest with over 86% current enrollment. Volta Region has the lowest enrollment rate, 80%, among these other seven regions. Ashanti, Central, Eastern, Brong Ahafo, and Western Regions show a near independent relationship because their enrollment rates ranged closely between 83 and 84%. Northern (51%), Upper East (59%), and Upper West (54%) Regions have the lowest range of participation rates.

The regional statistics reveal that Greater Accra, a traditionally patrilineal society, has the highest rate of school participation. As noted in Chapter Four, Greater Accra has many more accessible educational facilities than do the other regions, and is the ultimate destination for many migrants. Hence, unless specified, we cannot determine if respondents are Accra indigenes, i.e. the Ga ethnic group, or immigrants from other parts of the country or elsewhere. The three regions having lowest rates of school participation are all patrilineal. As the poorest in the country, they are the least attractive to migrants. Nevertheless, it is more reliable to blame the low rates of educational participation on poverty both at the household and regional levels, than on lineage.

Table 6.4: Mean Distribution of Regional Educational Participation

Regions	Mean	Frequency
Western	.9128	1,721
Central	.9240	1,395
Greater Accra	.9373	2,008
Volta	.8657	1,370
Eastern	.8990	1,951
Ashanti	.9180	2,623
Brong Ahafo	.8951	1,764
Northern	.5351	2,394
Upper East	.6222	1,027
Upper West	.5764	772
Total	.8243	17,025

Formal education in urban communities in Ghana is vastly different from what exists in rural regions. Usually the conditions of Ghana's urban public schools are not as deplorable as those in rural regions, making basic education more attractive to children of school-going age. Hence, it is easier for urban children in the research population to receive at least the basic education. Beyond the basic education, such children are less likely to end up in domestic servitude. Urban children who do not make it to traditional senior secondary schools are able to access alternatives which are hardly available in rural Ghana, e.g. commercial, vocational, or technical schools which are parallel to senior secondary schools but are terminal in the sense that their graduates learn skills in office administration, secretaryship, bookkeeping, carpentry, draftsmanship, and catering services and look for employment when they complete their training; even when available, rural parents might not be able to afford these alternatives.

From the discussions above we observe that both rural and urban children are at risk of child labor exploitation. However, given infrastructural availability and accessibility in urban, and to some extent semi-urban regions, rural children are

Table 6.5: Relationship between the Formal Educational Participation and Regions

	Western No. (%)	Central No. (%)	Greater Accra No. (%)	Volta No. (%)	Eastern No. (%)	Ashanti No. (%)	Brong Ahafo No. (%)	Northern No. (%)	Upper East No. (%)	Upper West No. (%)	Total No. (%)
None	150 (8.7)	106 6.3	126 6.3	184 (14)	197 (10)	215 (8)	185 (11)	1113 (47)	388 (38)	327 (43)	2991 (18)
Pre-S.*	205 (12)	157 (11)	164 (8.2)	106 (7.8)	80 (9)	245 (9)	203 (12)	68 (2.8)	16 (1.6)	49 (6.4)	1393 (8)
Primary	1056 (62)	832 (60)	11408 (57)	36 (61)	1201 (62)	1516 (58)	1089 (62)	1019 (43)	510 (50)	335 (44)	9524 (56)
J.S.S.**	281 (16)	275 (20)	473 (24)	235 (17)	339 (17)	588 (25)	259 (15)	169 (7)	102 (10)	55 (7)	2776 (16)
S.S.S.+	23 (1.3)	20 (1.4)	81 (4.1)	13 (1)	23 (1.2)	50 (1.9)	22 (1.3)	17 (.7)	7 (.7)	2 (.3)	258 (1.5)
Voc++	2 (.1)	2 (.1)	6 (.3)	2 (.1)	3 (.2)	4 (.2)	1 (.1)	0 (0)	2 (.2)	2 (.3)	24 (.1)
P.Sec+++	0 (0)	1 (.1)	0 (0)	0 (0)	0 (0)	0 (0)	0 (0)	0 (0)	0 (0)	0 (0)	1 (.0)
Total	1717 (100)	1393 (100)	1990 (100)	1366 (100)	1943 (100)	2,618 (100)	1759 (100)	2,386 (100)	1,025 (100)	770 (100)	16,967 (100)

Pearson Chi-Square (X2) = 3037.37   DF = 54   Sig. P = .000
Cramer's V = .173

*   Pre-school
**   Junior secondary school
+   Senior secondary school
++   Vocational training
+++ Post secondary training (nursing, teacher's training, school of agriculture)

more vulnerable to labor exploitation, comparatively. While low rates of enrollment and higher dropout rates exist among rural children, urban residents who are able to complete the basic education are also able to access other educational alternatives that make it possible for them to learn trades. Besides formal education, parental occupational and educational backgrounds as well as processes of socialization enshrined in some cultural practices determine the vulnerability of children to labor exploitation and slavery.

Table 6.6: Bivariate Association between Highest Level of Education and Type of Community (Rural or Urban)

	Urban		Rural		Total	
	No.	%	No.	%	No.	%
No Education	397	6.2	2,594	24.5	2,991	17.6
Pre-School	588	9.2	804	7.6	1,392	8.2
Primary	3,689	57.7	5,837	55.2	9,526	56.1
Junior Secondary	1,488	23.3	1,287	12.2	2,775	16.4
S.S.S. or higher	236	3.7	47	.4	283	1.7
Total	**6,398**	**100.0**	**10,569**	**100.0**	**16,967**	**100.0**

Pearson chi-square (X^2) = 1327.3   DF = 4   Sig. P = .000
Cramer's V = .280

Children in some cultures learn trades associated with their cultures or geographic locations. Rural children devote part of their time to working on farms or in fishing besides regular household chores that they have to perform. Boys and girls who are still enrolled in schools undergo these processes of socialization on weekends and after school on week days. Given that most villages do not have electricity, children of school-going age have very limited time to do school work when they return home from farming or fishing. During an undergraduate research project I conducted among a fishing community in the Central Region of Ghana, I discovered that fishing was more important than school to the children and their families, and, therefore, the people in that community refused to sacrifice daylight hours for children's school work. This problem is further compounded by the lack of educational facilities and teachers in rural Ghana. As a result, they perform badly in school even if they had adequate facilities and teachers to assist them in their studies. This partly explains why 60% of Ghana's rural school children, as pointed out in Chapter Two, have received no basic literacy (see Berlan, 2004).

RELATIONSHIP BETWEEN FORMAL EDUCATIONAL PARTICIPATION AND CHILD DOMESTIC SERVITUDE

From the above information gained through my research, we observe that formal education is not equally accessible to Ghanaian children. The inability of parents to afford educational expenses even in the face of the FCUBE and the need for some children to travel to nearby communities to go to school, at times, make formal education less attractive to both parents and children. These factors also make child domestic servitude a lucrative venture among rural families. In the following paragraphs, I discuss these relationships in detail.

I observed from the qualitative data that there are a number of domestic servants who graduate from the junior secondary school (J.S.S.) and go into domestic servitude as a means of accumulating the necessary resources to go into some type of apprentice training, usually dressmaking or hairdressing. A very limited number of them go to school while living in servitude. There were others also who either dropped out of school or never enrolled at all. They also see domestic servitude as a means of escaping rural life and learning a trade.

There were 16 current domestic servants who had dropped out of school, while 18 had completed the J.S.S. Three of them were still in school. Seven current domestic servants never went to school. The oldest person in this sample, the 28-year-old woman I met at one of the two employment agencies that I discussed in Chapter Four, was also the only domestic servant respondent who had completed the senior secondary school (S.S.S.). The second oldest person was 25 years old and was recruited at the age of 15 and dropped out of school.

The younger generation of former domestic servants was more educated relative to their older counterparts. Only one of the eight post-1980 former domestic servants dropped out of school and the rest had completed the J.S.S. Some of them attained or were about to attain their long term goal of becoming hairdressers or dressmakers. Only one of them had completed her training as a dressmaker at the time of this research. Funded by her mother, Samira had gone back to school and was in her final year at a fashion institute. Only one of them had become pregnant. The rest were in training to become hairdressers or dressmakers.

Based on the observation that child domestic servants were almost always out of school during servitude, this research concludes that education seems to be a major means to ending or alleviating child labor exploitation. We observe also that children who successfully complete the J.S.S. might use domestic servitude as a stepping stone to learning trades that will advance and enhance their independence as adults. This study, therefore, asked the research question: *what is the relationship between formal educational participation and child domestic servitude*? This question sought to determine the role that education plays in the incidence of child labor in general and tested the hypothesis below.

Hypothesis Test 4: Bivariate Association between Formal School Participation and Child Labor

H_0 = no association exists between formal school participation of children and child labor;

H_1 = an association exists between formal school participation of children and child labor.

The dependent variable of child workers consisting of all children who were younger than 18 years (regardless of their relationship to the head of household) was cross-tabulated with formal education. According to Table 6.7, as many as 90% of children who have never been to school, 90% of those who are still attending school, and nearly 84% who left school live with their own parents or grandparents. Only 8% of those who never attended school, 7% of those still attending school, and 12% of those who left school already live with other parents. Given a Pearson chi-square (X^2) (4; N = 16,742) of 112 (.000), this relationship is statistically significant at α = .05. A Cramer's V score of .08 indicates, however, that the association between formal education and child labor, considering all child workers including those who live with their parents and grandparents, is a very weak one.

Table 6.7: Bivariate Association between Formal Educational Participation and Child Workers (Including Those Who Live with Own Parents)

	Never Attended		Attended Still attending		Past (Left School)		Total	
	No.	%	No.	%	No.	%	No.	%
Child/Grandchild	2,629	90.0	11,791	91.8	815	83.5	15,235	91.0
Other Relative	238	8.2	904	7.0	116	11.9	1,258	7.5
Non-Relative	53	1.8	151	1.2	45	4.6	249	1.5
Total	2,920	100.0	12,846	100.0	976	100.0	16,742	100.0

Pearson chi-square (X^2) = 112   DF = 4   Sig. P = .000
Cramer's V = .08

The dominance of children living with their parents or grandparents—either as current students, past students, or children who were never enrolled—is probably a reflection of the pattern of respondents' relationship to the household heads in the data. A majority of the respondents in this research live with their own parents, and it is more likely for them to go to school than for those who live with non-parents. In order to control for this dominance of children who live with their parents in the determination of the association between child work and participation of children in formal education, the dependent variable of child servants which excludes children who live with their parents and grandparents was cross-tabulated with children's schooling.

The findings are presented in Table 6.8. Nearly 82% of all servants who never attended school live with other relatives while 18% of them live with non-relatives. Of those who are attending school, 86% live with relatives, 14% live with non-relatives, 72% of those who left school live with relatives while 28% of them live with non-relatives. In this test the incidence of children living with relatives tends to be high, and this holds true whether the child was never enrolled in school, was currently enrolled or had left. These findings do not provide sufficient evidence to support the hypothesis given a Pearson chi-square (X^2) of (2, N = 1507) of 19.6 (.000). Hence the H_0 of no association between formal education and child labor/servitude is rejected at α = .05. Moreover, there is a weak relationship between child servitude and formal education given a Cramer's V score of .114.

Table 6.8: Bivariate Association between Formal Educational Participation and Child Servants (Excluding Those Who Live with Own Parents)

Relationship to Household Head	Never Attended		Attended/ Still attending		Past (Left School)		Total	
	No.	%	No.	%	No.	%	No.	%
Other Relative	238	81.8	904	85.7	116	72.0	1,258	83.5
Non-Relative	53	18.2	151	14.3	45	28.0	249	16.5
Total	291	100.0	1,055	100.0	161	100.0	1,507	100.0

Pearson chi-square (X^2) = 19.58   DF = 2   Sig. P = .000
Cramer's V = .114

RELATIONSHIP BETWEEN LINEAGE, FORMAL EDUCATION, AND CHILD LABOR EXPLOITATION

While the following tests are similar to the above, they differ in that they focused on the relationship between lineage, formal education, and the incidence of child labor. The first test, which follows the above, examines the relationship between matrilineage and patrilineage on one hand and formal education on the other. Earlier in Chapter Five, I controlled for regions given that ethnic groups are usually conglomerations of many regions and also for the argument that some regions were more endowed with social amenities and infrastructure than others.

Hypothesis Test 5: Bivariate Association between Lineage and Formal School Participation of Children

H_0 = no association exists between lineage and formal school participation of children;

H_1 = an association exists between lineage and formal school participation of children.

As Table 6.9 illustrates, there exists an association between formal education and lineage in Ghana. The data shows that children from matrilineal ethnic groups in general are more likely to go to school than those from patrilineal backgrounds. A total of 17.7% of children from both matrilineal and patrilineal backgrounds do not go to school. However, only 5.7% of matrilineal and 27.4% of patrilineal children never attended school. A little over 76.4% of all children are enrolled in school. Among children from matrilineal backgrounds, a little over 87.2% are enrolled in schools, while 67.5% of patrilineal ethnic groups are enrolled in school. A Pearson chi-square (X^2) ((2, N = 16412) of 1313.46 (.000) establishes that there is a relationship between lineage and school enrollment among children in Ghana. This finding is statistically significant at α = .05. The hypothesis of no association is thus rejected. A Cramer's V of .283 indicates, however, that the strength of this relation, although significant, is less than moderate.

The same hypothesis, (i.e. H_0 = no association exists between lineage and formal school participation of children, H_1 = an association exists between lineage and formal school participation of children) was tested using the highest level of education attained by respondents as the dependent variable. Given a Pearson chi-square (X^2) (6, N = 16,354) of 1441.46 (.000), the data evidence a statistically significant bivariate association between lineage and educational attainment. As Table 6.10 suggests, the largest number of children are either in the primary school or they drop out at that level. The test of bivariate relationship between educational attainment and lineage reveals that 60% of matrilineal and 52% of patrilineal children who are aged between five and 17 are either in the primary school or drop out at that level. Together they constitute nearly 60% of all children aged below 18 but who are at least five years old.

Table 6.9: Bivariate Association between Lineage and School Participation

Status of Enrollment	Matrilineal No.	%	Patrilineal No	%	Total No.	%
Never attended	421	5.7	2,476	27.4	2,900	17.7
Still attending	6,437	87.2	6,098	67.5	12,532	76.4
Past/left	524	7.1	456	5.0	980	6.0
Total	7,382	100.0	9,030	100.0	16,412	100.0

Pearson chi-square (X^2) = 1313.46   DF = 2   Sig. P = .000
Cramer's V = .283

Table 6.10: Bivariate Association between Lineage and School Attainment

Education	Matrilineal No.	%	Patrilineal No.	%	Total No.	%
No Education	424	5.8	2,476	27.5	2,900	17.7
Pre-School	795	10.8	549	6.1	1,344	8.2
Primary	4,415	60.0	4,732	52.6	9,147	55.9
Middle/JSS	1,566	21.3	1,123	12.5	2,689	16.4
Secondary/SSS	149	2.0	103	1.1	252	1.5
Voc/Tech/Commercial	9	.1	12	.1	21	.1
Post secondary*	1	0	0	0	1	0
Total	7,359	100.0	8,995	100.0	16,354	100.0

Pearson chi-square (X^2) = 1441.33 DF = 6   Sig. P = .000
Cramer's V = .297

*(Agricultural/Nursing/Teacher training)

CHAPTER SUMMARY AND CONCLUSION

This chapter analyzes the relationship between formal education and the incidence of child domestic servitude in Ghana. It gives an overview of the structures of education in Ghana and shows that children who are most vulnerable to domestic labor exploitation are those who complete basic school without advancing to high school or drop out without graduating. Existing research indicates that girls are more likely to drop out of school than boys. As Michael Kevane (2004) notes, girls are more likely to leave school to work because their parents consider them to be more generous with their incomes (Kevane, 2004; Mikay, 1997). In many cultures of the research population, when resources are scarce, girls were less likely to remain in school because of the belief that they would one day end up as housewives. Parental educational backgrounds and their occupations are also important factors that determine school participation of children. I argued in this chapter that highly educated parents had good jobs and so could afford to fund their children's education. Finally, I noted that urban children had more access to formal education and so are less likely to be exploited in domestic servitude.

Chapter VIII

CHILD DOMESTIC SERVITUDE: THE QUESTION ON CONTEMPORARY SLAVERY

Chapter One of this inquiry presents conclusions that the research draws about the processes of recruitment, methods of remuneration of domestic services, and how such payment is put to use. These observations were located in theory to determine if the domestic servants who participated in this research are in fact slaves. This chapter is a presentation of the findings regarding the statuses of the domestic servants vis-à-vis slavery.

I organized the theories from the literature into two categories, namely those that explain old slavery and those that currently explain and define contemporary slavery. Theories explaining old forms or traditional slavery emphasize permanent ownership of the slaves, their transferability, high levels of profitability, and the fact that old slavery was legally permitted. From the limited literature on contemporary slavery, I considered processes of recruitment, the level of maturity, and ability of the domestic servants to give consent to their recruitment and assigned responsibilities. In summary, the use of force and violent control of the victims' labor (Bales, 2000; 1999) and their lack of consent and maturity (Barry, 1984) are the basic characteristics of contemporary slavery that this research looked for in the domestic servants. Additionally, I employed prior distinction between positive and negative children's work, which I outlined in my MA thesis, to critically assess the position of my respondents. In both Convention 182 (*Eliminating the Worst Forms of Child Labor*) and the Practical Guide to that Convention (*The Handbook for Parliamentarians No. 3: Eliminating the Worst Forms of Child*

Labor), the ILO describes positive children's work as functional to their socialization, personal and economic developments, and to their families.

Although the processes of their recruitment did not make the domestic servants in this research slaves, a majority of the current and former domestic servants, some of their employers, the parents and the Director of Ghana's Social Welfare did confirm that some of them live under de facto conditions of slavery. They are physically and verbally abused, they are not paid, some of them cannot go back to their parents for fear of being sent back, and most importantly, they do not have their free will while living as domestic servants in other households. Although I could not define them as contemporary slaves, I categorized them as quasi-slaves because they are not free laborers, and some of them are not even mature or knowledgeable enough to give informed consent.

DOMESTIC SERVANTS WHO ARE NOT CONTEMPORARY SLAVES

Going by conventional processes of obtaining slaves, this research could have defined eight of the current and former domestic servants among the respondents as slaves. These are respondents who were too young to be knowledgeable about domestic servitude and to be able to consent to their employment. The use of force characteristic of slavery acquisition in general, however, is non-existent among the rest of the domestic servants. They were usually aware of the potential exploitation and abuses that domestic servants sometimes encountered. In fact some of them had accepted domestic servitude positions three or four times prior to their current or most immediate recruitments. Their awareness or previous experiences in servitude and its inherent abuses could not stop them from remaining in or reentering servitude; most of these servants are driven to live in servitude by severe economic conditions and cultural expectations. They are the quasi-slaves. I conceptualize the quasi-slaves of Ghana's domestic servitude as persons who, although obtained through what might be described as acceptable means of recruitment, suffer verbal and physical abuses, stand a high probability of not being able to leave servitude for fear of losing their accrued incomes or for the lack of the freedom to do so, and who generally suffer forms of slavery-like exploitations and abuses.

The youngest of my respondents was Hawa, the-eight-year-old shop keeper whose paternal uncle sent her into domestic servitude. Using Barry's definition alone, I could qualify Hawa as a contemporary slave in its absolute terms. Becoming a domestic servant at the age of six, this servant was indisputably too young to be working as a shop attendant. Nevertheless, this research could not define her as an absolute slave because of the circumstances surrounding her recruitment and the answers that she provided regarding her reasons for being there. My interview with her uncle and recruiter also gave indispensable pointers to my understanding of Hawa's position.

According to her employee/uncle, sending Hawa into domestic servitude was her father's approach to securing her economic independence. Hawa had never attended school because her father could not afford it. Her stay with her parents might not have made life any worse for them; however, she would have remained out of school with no hope of learning a trade some time in the future. Therefore, when her father sent her into domestic servitude, he was looking for an avenue that would ensure that his daughter would eventually learn a trade and become economically independent in adulthood.

Furthermore, Hawa did not experience any of the enslaving treatments that other servants had to endure. Hawa understood why she was working for the shop owner. She told me that she was there to help her for a period of time and at the end of her service provided the means to learn a trade. Her employer affirmed this, stating that she was committed to sending Hawa into an apprentice training program when the time came. As this case and those to be discussed below exemplify, families intend for their children to attain certain skills that will move them forward in their personal and economic growth. However, the fact remains that this poor child is not a beneficiary of some of the numerous rights enjoyed by many children; most importantly she lost her childhood to poverty and thus did not experience the joy of living with her own parents. Unfortunately, it is a catch-22 situation for these domestic servants.

Lily is another young respondent who shared a similar economic background to Hawa. She was also six at the time of her recruitment. Lily's mother made the request for her daughter to become a domestic servant in the employer's house-hold in Accra. She had already spent six years in that household when I met her. According to this employer, she accepted their offer to have Lily live with her primarily because she needed someone to keep her mother company. Soon after her recruitment, the employer sent her to school.

Unlike Hawa, who appeared so content with her new household, Lily wept intermittently during the interview because she missed her mother so much. When asked if she wished she were back home with her parents and siblings, she responded in the negative, explaining that her mother "could not feed" her. Conclusively, her mother could not finance her formal education. Like Hawa, even at such a young age, Lily understood the circumstances surrounding her stay with a different family in Accra. In addition, she understood the discriminatory treatment that her employer gave her vis-à-vis her grandchildren. As she pointed out, she wished she could play like the other children but could not do so when her employer was at home. Like Hawa, Lily lost her childhood to poverty, although in her case she was fortunate to receive formal education.

In a follow-up call to Ghana, I learned that Lily's employer had sent her back to her parents for petty thievery. They described the scene of her return as pathetic because she cried bitterly, refusing to stay behind. After a few weeks when the employer visited that town again, she found Lily in a miserable condition; she had dropped out of school and was washing dishes with her mother in exchange for food. Out of pity, this employer took her back to Accra so she could reenroll her in school.

Given that economic independence and growth for Lily and Hawa was contingent on their stay with other families, and given also that they were not abused and forced to work under violent threats, I could not classify them as contemporary slaves in absolute terms. This observation notwithstanding, we cannot disagree with the fact that these two young girls have been denied their childhood, do not live in families that necessarily give them the love and care that they need, and they have been denied the right to live with their own parents. These attributes also characterize the domestic servants who were recruited before the age of 13.

In addition to these servants, there were some young adults who were mature and knowledgeable enough to consent to their recruitment and assignment into domestic servitude and thus could be classified neither as contemporary nor quasi-slaves. Nonetheless, they are also victims of the labor-repressive system under discussion. They are exploited labor. Derrick's recruits, most of whom had completed the basic education, satisfied this level of knowledgeability and could negotiate their incomes with their employers and recruiter. Moreover, they had received the basic education and so had that right provided, usually by their own parents. Inarguably, they are victims of exploitation in the sense of working long hours without a commensurate level of remuneration, if paid at all. Many of these victims of exploitation seemed content with their statuses as domestic servants. One of them is Serwah.

I spoke to Serwah in one of the teacher's bungalows in a Kumasi-based secondary school. She was very pleasant. She told me she was very happy that she had agreed to come to the city. I visited her small village of about 320 residents but could not get her mother to interview. This small village had no pipe-borne water, and residents had to walk about two miles to nearby streams to get water. Except for a small wooden kiosk where a woman sold a few canned foods and fried yams, there were no shops or markets. Residents carried their farm produce to the roadside to sell to motorists who cared to stop. There were no hospitals or health posts. The highest class in the only school was the sixth grade, and children had to walk if their parents could not afford the transport fare to the nearest town to go to school. Parents who were better off, and there were just about four households at that, did not allow their children to start the primary school in this village at all. As a parent told me, teachers in this school hardly reported to teach.

Considering this type of community where she originally lived, I understood why Serwah was so pleasant towards me and happy that she had migrated to the city. When Serwah's recruiter consulted the former's mother to ask permission for her daughter to go and live in Kumasi, she received her approval. When asked what she would have done if the mother had refused to allow her to travel, Serwah indicated that she would have run away. She was very pleased with her employer, although she had never been paid for her services. There were many other current domestic servants who were very pleased to be living in other households in the cities, the lack of pay notwithstanding. Given their level of content, maturity, and the fact that they had received basic education in most cases, I concluded that they were neither contemporary nor quasi-slaves but exploited labor.

CONTEMPORARY SLAVERY: PERCEPTIONS OF SOME DOMESTIC SERVANTS

The domestic servants discussed above are not contemporary slaves in absolute terms. Unfortunately, I could not say the same thing for every respondent in this research. Some of them wept mercilessly while narrating their abusive experiences in domestic servitude. They wished they could return home, but some of their parents would not permit it. In this subsection, I discuss some of the domestic servants that this research identifies as contemporary slaves. As stated earlier, I relate the domestic servants' experiences, the methods and beneficiaries of pay, whether or not they are able to willingly exit contemporary slavery to definitions of slavery in general, and those of contemporary slavery in particular.

As Esi's father explained when I paid him a visit in his hometown, she was his daughter, and if she returned home today, he was going to send her back the next day. Esi was 18 at the time of this research and, as a young adult, could have voluntarily left this family, but her father's decision was final. This parental decision-making role in such instances was almost universal among these respondents. Serena is another domestic servant whose living and working conditions confirmed her as a contemporary slave. She was only five the first time she lived with someone. This was with an extended family member who lived alone with the respondent. Serena started school while living with this woman. She kept her extended relative's small convenience stall when she got home from school. She had to return to her mother because this woman's boyfriend left her and thieves broke into the stall, making away with the wares. Serena's current employer came to see her mother in the company of another woman, probably a recruiter, but she could not tell. This employer promised to send her back to school, but she should live with her for some time. Serena said the time promised had already passed, but there had not been any mention of her going back to school.

She kept a convenience store in front of the woman's home, a compound house that she shared with several other families. She wept throughout this interview. She wished she could go back home but could not tell her employer. She was waiting for her mother to visit one day so she would make her aware of the treatment she was enduring. Unfortunately, she had no contact with her mother and at 17 could not find her way to her mother's home. What upset her most was her employer's husband's incessant verbal abuses whenever she refused to give him part of the sales. Usually, he referred to her as a slave who had been given to them as a gift. There were four children in this household. The oldest was 23 and the youngest 12. They were either in school or learning a trade.

Selasie is another servant this research identified as a contemporary slave. At 13 years of age, she did not know her parents and could not tell where she had come from. The only thing she knows about herself is the fact that she is an Ewe, given that she speaks the Ewe language. That, however, is her employer's native language too and so it is possible she learned it from her; she came to live with her when she was about three years old. Selasie has nowhere to go should she decide to leave servitude. In the first place, she does not have her actual family's background, and in the second, she is a minor and so cannot become independent without finding herself on the streets. Selasie looked and behaved far younger than her 13 years, she was timid and withdrawn during my interactions with her. In the interview, she told me about the physical abuses that she suffered from her employer. Unlike other servants though, she could tell me all her experiences without shedding a tear. I assumed that having lived and experienced such abuses from so young an age without knowing how it felt like to live in a loving family, she had no past memories of kindness to use as a reference and thus could not relate the nostalgic feelings that other domestic servants were able to share about their families and villages.

Two of these three domestic servants, Selasie and Serena, qualified as contemporary slaves because of the processes of their recruitment. Most of the other servants, as well as Esi and these two, were enslaved through their working conditions, the treatment they received from their employers, and the fact that they cannot exit servitude. Like Esi, nearly all respondents in this research, including employers and the two government officials I interviewed, identified the way employers and their families treated domestic servants as enslaving. The domestic servants further expressed the fear that their employers may not put them through any skill training before or after they leave servitude.

When asked if they considered themselves or domestic servants (in the case of non-domestic servant respondents) to be slaves (or to explain who a slave is), a majority of domestic servants, employers, and recruiters responded in the affirmative but with an emphasis on the treatment meted out to some of them. The following are some of the responses from some current domestic servants:

Esi: I sometimes feel I have no one, but when I visit my sister, she talks to me... I don't have my peace and freedom in this house, but when I visit my sister, she understands my pain and worries, so she is usually able to comfort me.

Mansah: It is so pathetic the way children who live with other families are treated.... Yes, some of them are.... They hit the slave with anything they could lay hands on—shoes, spatula—and when their children speak, the slave should not be around. The woman's children could ask you to hand-wash their underwear for them, the woman herself could give you her underwear to wash. These things make you a slave.

Kate: They are [slaves] since they also serve, but we've referred to them as house-girls so… someone who has been brought to work [pauses] around the house.

Joy: Like they're living with people whom they have bought.

Anna: Oh, those who live with other families … given that the children live with them, they make slaves out of them. The 'hosts' can do anything with the child living with them.

Emelia: To me they are not… the Bible says if your sister is in difficulty, help her…some people will tell you they will help you, but when you live with them, they maltreat you…

Gladys: Not that they are slaves, but if you consider the way that they are treated, you might think they are slaves… they treat their children differently from their helpers, and what their children would do that won't attract any punishment, the helper would be punished for the same offense.

Paulyn: Someone who is assigned work that she can't do.

Paula: Those who live with some people… she lives with somebody and works for the person.

Stephanie: Some families are poor and … they help those with money so they will support them. So when you do anything bad and they insult you, they tell you that you are a servant or a slave…

Angela: Hmmm, I can't say that we are slaves because as human beings, I am a slave of God's… we are slaves for sure… because we are treated as though you are not a part of the human race, that you weren't born. But our parents suffered the same way as the others to bring us forth, but because of something.

Rita: Someone who lives with other families.

Edna: Some of them… there are those parents who do not let their children do anything in the house. It is the child who lives with them who does everything. This makes the child a slave.

Ingrid: Some of them… it means that the person they live with doesn't treat them like her own children.

Former domestic servants expressed it thusly:

Patricia: She treated me in a way that made me feel I was not hu-
                       man... because I served them ... a slave, I think is someone
                       who has been brought to serve another person or groups of
                       persons.

Helene: Yes some people are... like a maid... someone who helps with
                       household chores, etc... yes, the woman made me a maid.

Margaret: It all depends on how you are treated. Some people could
                       take you to be their own children. So it is all dependent on
                       the attitude of the person who lives with you.

Samira: Someone who lives with somebody and serves that person.
                       Such a servant is made to do things or go places where their
                       own children will not be allowed to go.

While the processes of recruitment are generally significant in the conceptualization of any slavery relationships, these responses reflect Kopytoff's ideas on the
processes of dehumanization and rehumanization. Although these responses do not
support the notion of dehumanization, which starts from the moment the domestic
servant is recruited, respondents agree that, after recruitment, they are indeed dehumanized. As discussed in the introductory chapter, domestic servants lose their identities as daughters, sisters, students, or family members and therefore have to reorient
themselves about their statuses. They have to learn new attributes that come with
their new identities as domestic servants. For instance, they must realize that they
cannot go to bed because they are sleepy—they can do that only when they complete
their chores for the day. Additionally, they cannot sleep in like the rest of the family—in this case also, they have to get up earlier than anybody else because they have
chores to do. There are instances also where domestic servants cannot eat when they
are hungry because instructions to eat have to come from their employers.

One cannot help but wonder though why they remain in servitude or accept
re-assignment if they consider their employers' treatment of them to be enslavement. I found my answer in a simple response by Angela who had lost both parents, "...we are after something," she said. The pursuit of that "something" (exposure to city life and common etiquette, skill training and reduction in the level
of household dependency on their families) could go on unabated until they derive
optimum satisfaction and utility (see Kevane, 2004) from their stay as domestic
servants with other families.

Child domestic servitude and other forms of child labor existed prior to the
onset of neo-liberal economic policies in Ghana. While it is true that harsh economic realities facing Ghanaian families and women in particular as a result of
unfavorable neo-liberal economic policies cause some children to end up in child

domestic servitude and consequently contemporary slavery, I observed that for the participants in this research, unless the domestic servant is too young to decide for herself, what sustains this practice are their expectations of gains and rewards. These expectations also direct the processes of recruitment. They will continue to accept offers of recruitment in so far as they believe in the potential benefits of living with other families in the cities.

CHAPTER SUMMARY AND CONCLUSION

This research adopted definitions in the literature about slavery in general and contemporary slavery in particular. Important among the attributes of contemporary slavery is the nature of exploitation—whether or not they are old enough to be able to consent to their employment, if they receive any pay at all, and if they can voluntarily leave servitude. The juxtaposition of the theories and experiences of domestic servants as discussed above lead to two major conclusions. In the first place, I conclude that many child domestic servants in Ghana are not contemporary slaves in absolute terms but quasi-slaves. In the second place, I observe the cultural practicality of child domestic servitude, this being observable in the training that respondents claim they receive in housekeeping, etiquette, and apprenticeship.

Most of the participants in this research were old enough to accept job offers. They had attained the basic education and were at least 15 years old, which is the minimum age of employment in Ghana. Without the influence of their parents or any adult, some girls voluntarily dropped out of school before becoming domestic servants. Such school dropouts in fact looked forward to the opportunity to become domestic servants in the cities. It is in regards to the fact that school dropouts in Ghana use domestic servitude as a means of acquiring their economic independence during adulthood that I conclude that this type of child labor is culturally practical but only to the extent that the children would be provided the chance to acquire some type of trade.

My observation that this would help socialize children and to keep them busy while they stay out of school, notwithstanding, I do agree with my respondents that although they are not acquired through slavery means, the way they are treated while living with their employers tends to be enslaving. That most of them are not paid substantiates this observation.

In answering the question on the beneficiary of their incomes, the data exonerate their parents or families from the assumption that they sell or give their children away into contemporary slavery in order that the families would survive. Contrary to Moore's exclusion of the exploitation of family labor from slavery, I would have defined these respondents as slaves if their families were usurping their incomes. As it turns out, the definition of these domestic servants as slaves is restricted to their in-service experiences.

Chapter IX

CONCLUSIONS: HISTORICAL AND DOMESTIC AND ECONOMIC EXPLANATIONS OF CONTEMPORARY CHILD DOMESTIC SERVITUDE

Child domestic servitude exists in Ghana today primarily because there is a huge demand for it. This demand, according to the two theories of survival strategies that partially guided this research, exists because of worsening conditions of poverty in both rural and urban regions. Usually, child domestics originate from rural Ghana and live with households in urban or semi-urban communities. Contrary to newspaper reports and prior research about child labor in other parts of the world, children who work as domestic servants are neither sold nor obtained through trafficking. Instead, a majority of them voluntarily drop out of school and either look for potential employers or accept offers from recruiters who will help them migrate to the cities to work as domestic servants. This study also discovered that contrary to my pre-research expectations, a large number of domestic servants in Ghana are older than the minimum working age, and they often complete the basic education before entering domestic servitude. I concluded from the qualitative data that cotemporary child domestic servitude evolved from a historical practice of children living with newly-married female members of their extended families in order to provide free domestic services, and in exchange, received training in some type of trade, housekeeping skills, and in some cases formal education.

REASONS FOR THE CONTINUED EXISTENCE OF CHILD DOMESTIC SERVITUDE IN GHANA

As noted earlier, the CRC requires that children remain in school until the minimum working age and also that they be provided with some skills that will enable them become useful and independent members of society in adulthood. Like the CRC, the Convention for the Elimination of Worst Forms of Child Labor calls on party states to protect their children from harmful employment and those that would inhibit their successful socialization and physiological growth. Given the role of the Minimum Age Convention, the stipulations of all other conventions protecting children from labor exploitation should be successful. However, this has not been the case. This research outlined some of the factors that have thwarted the efficacy of these conventions.

I noted in Chapter Two that flexibilities in the Minimum Age Convention invariably sanction the exploitation of children under certain circumstances while protecting them from others. I suggested that in view of the fact that the lack of educational resources and infrastructure can cause children to take longer than normal to complete the basic education, permitting low income countries to lower the minimum working age, means the licensing of the children's exploitation. In addition, although international law requires party states to ensure that children develop into independent adults, their preparation for adult roles are costly, and poor countries are not always able to finance their education.

Child domestic servitude exists because of economic and cultural reasons. Indisputably, it is a form of survival strategy for both the child's family and the family into which the child domestic servant is hired. To the hiring family, the domestic servant is a means of cheap or free labor for petty trading and for household chores. The domestic servant's family, on the other hand, perceives domestic servitude not as a means of its own survival, as part of the literature purports, but as a means of helping their younger female members to become independent and useful adults. Households in urban and semi-urban areas are those who usually hire domestic servants. Depending on occupations of the heads of such households, the domestic servant would be engaged exclusively in petty trading or in household chores. More often than not, domestic servants, this research discovered, combine the two types of responsibilities.

I observed that approach used to analyze domestic servitude; these responsibilities corroborate the MML theory of survival strategy that urban households have had to rely on multiple sources of income following continual economic erosion that resulted from unsuccessful neo-liberal economic policies. They either earn incomes through domestic servants' duties of selling for their employers or through the savings that the households make by not hiring adult domestics while female heads undertake professional careers outside the home.

In semi-urban communities that have some social amenities and infrastructure, such as high schools and hospitals, domestic servants usually sell cooked food, keep convenience stores of their employers, and at times take care of household chores if the family does not have a second servant. In urban communities also, domestic servants combine household chores with petty trading for their employers. As I observed, the difference between semi-urban and urban employers lies in their respective levels of education and type of primary occupations. Self-employed petty traders, the data showed, are more likely to employ domestic servants for commercial activities. Employers with multiple sources of income also assign domestic workers to petty trading. In order for such households to enjoy the services of domestic servants in both their businesses and around the house, some employers choose to have more than one domestic servant. Afriyie's and Hawa's employers discussed in the preceding chapters are two examples.

For working 10 to 16 hours a day, the working conditions of Ghana's domestic servants may not be considered appalling if they receive remunerations commensurate with the amount of work done. Many domestic servants, as earlier discussions in this book point out, do not get paid for the services that they provide. In order for them to get paid, domestic servants who participated in this study have to overstay the agreed period of two to three years. According to the data, those who receive payments without staying the entire duration are usually recruits of non-formal agents of recruitment. The cash payment or the training that those who get paid receive is often not commensurate with the child domestics' work. The highest paid non-formally or informally recruited current domestic servant received C80,000 (approximately $7.00) a month for working 10 to 16 hours a day.

Others choose to pay their servants off at the end of their service. The usual means of payment is an enrollment in an apprenticeship, either to become a hairdresser or seamstress. At the time of recruitment, employers usually arrange with families, or the servants themselves, the method of payment and how much it should be. On average, employers agree to enroll them in the apprenticeship after two years of service. The entry fees ranged between C200.000 and C1 million. Employers must also get their recruits sewing machines and the necessary tools to start the training. Even when employers provide these after the two year period of service in addition to the domestic servant's living expenses, they probably would not be justified for underpaying or not paying the servants.

The sending families also gain from their younger members' engagement in domestic servitude. However, this research concludes that such benefits are mostly non-fiscal. First, the sending families do not have to take care of another dependent. Secondly, if successful, the domestic servant will return home financially ready to start learning a trade, an indication that the family will not have to struggle about the younger member's future economic security. On rare occasions, servants who receive cash for their services remit part of it to their families back home. In this research, only one respondent, Akosua, sent an equivalent of a month's wage to her mother who was taking care of the former's son.

Domestic servants usually request either their employers or recruiters to save their incomes until the end of their service period when they collect the bulk sum for their training. The family's hope of seeing their younger member return home ready to learn a trade may be squashed if for any reason the daughter decides to leave servitude prematurely. This research observed that servants at times left servitude before the contract period ends when they considered their employers' homes to be too quiet. There were other participants who left employers' homes because they had stayed too long and were not expecting their employers to pay them off soon enough. When servants leave under such circumstances, they most always lose their accumulated incomes. Employers told me that even when they do not pay or enroll domestic servants into training, we cannot conclude that the servants are not paid at all since they provided the servants' basic needs and covered their medical expenses.

BECOMING DOMESTIC SERVANTS

I identified three different approaches of recruitment and classified them as formal, non-formal, and informal. Formal recruiters were registered employment agencies which specialize in the recruitment of domestic workers, house-boys, garden-boys, and cooks. These employment agencies receive applications from both domestic servants and households looking for helpers. Informal recruiters are neither registered nor regular. They are the occasional intermediaries between prospective domestic servants and their employers. There were three different types of informal recruiting. The first type involves family members who assist relatives in either recruiting or becoming domestic servants. The second type involves non-family members, while the third is a combination of both family and non-family members.

Although different from the two other types of recruiters, non-formal agents exhibit traits of both formal and informal recruiters. They are regular recruiters who, although not formally established as agents of recruitment, bring children from rural areas to live with and work for other families. Like the informal processes of recruitment, they employ children of all ages, making these domestic servants vulnerable to various forms of abuses and exploitation. The non-formal recruiters receive no payment for their services, except for the reimbursement of their travel expenses when employers send them to the villages.

I observed a number of similarities and differences among Sophia's and Derrick's recruitment patterns, on the one hand, and those of Ali and Ahmed on the other. Unlike Derrick's and Sophia's, Ali's and Ahmed's recruits lived in less developed towns with petty traders who needed them not only to work around the house but also to hawk and/or keep small shops. Another difference is the educational and economic backgrounds of their employers. Whereas employers at Tikobo #1 and Bonyere where Ali and Ahmed served, respectively, were primarily semi-educated, low income earners who lived off petty trading, those at Accra, and Cape Coast where Derrick and Sophia served, were highly educated university professors and businessmen who had better economic standing and social class.

The period of stay for Ali's and Ahmed's recruits ranged between two and three years. Three factors most likely responsible for the low recruit turnover for Ali and Ahmed are the cultural backgrounds of their recruits and their similarities with their destinations. There is a general notion among Ghanaians that the northerner is the most subservient of all the tribal groups in the country. They could tolerate those abuses and contempt characteristic of domestic servitude in general, which the girls from the south could not endure for long. The second factor is the similarities between the hometowns and Tikobo #1 and the surrounding villages. The northern part of Ghana is the least developed in the country and thus exhibited much of the rural attributes that characterized Tikobo #1. Among these characteristics is the lack of individualism that domestic servants at Accra and Cape Coast encountered. Recruits to Accra usually complain of the quiet neighborhoods and curtailed their contracts as a result. The third factor is the lack of competitiveness in the rural areas.

I observed three different scenarios as far as relationships among recruiters, employers, and domestic servants and their families were concerned. These are the non-familial relationship, the kin-group relationship, and the shared-solidarity relationship. The pattern of non-familial relationship exists where domestic servants worked for total strangers who come from and live in different parts of the country, and have someone look for a helper from the rural area for them. I categorized the relationship between a domestic servant and her employer as the kin-group relationship if they are related by blood or through marriage. Extended family members fall under this category. Out of 44 current domestic servants, seven lived with blood relations and only one of them was male. My pre-research expectation that domestic servants who lived with relatives would be least abused proved to be wrong for the respondents in this research.

The shared-solidarity relationship existed when domestic servants and their employers originate from the same village or hometown. There were six respondents who came from the same hometowns as the female heads (i.e. the wives of the male heads) of the households in which they lived. I observed that this attitude of shared-solidarity creates some sense of commitment in female household heads who are directly responsible for the domestic servants. Even when highly dissatisfied with the domestic servant's performance, employers who came from the same hometown as their servants were more willing to provide some type of remuneration than those from different hometowns.

THEORETICAL IMPLICATIONS
OF THIS RESEARCH

This investigation sought to fill the existent void in current literature on child domestic servants in Ghana. Before going to the field, there had not been any scholarly publication on child domestic servants in Ghana. Thus, this study was primarily exploratory. It focused on discovering the recruitment processes, working conditions, procedures of exiting from servitude, and methods of payment and disbursement of the servants' incomes. The sampling techniques which I employed in this research sought to overcome the problems, that according to the literature, characterized research on children who work within the household. The survey technique was not effective in identifying domestic servants because of the issue of mistaking them as the children of household heads.

As noted earlier, this research confirmed observation in the literature that child labor in general exists because of poverty. However, it refutes the theory that some families' survival depends on incomes from their children's work. This research discovered that families encourage their children to work because of the belief that it might possibly be the only means through which the children could become independent and useful adults in society. I observed from the participants in this research that families usually have no access to the incomes that their children generate from their domestic servitude.

Existing research on child domestic servitude illustrates relationships between gender and child domestic servitude. In some societies, girls are restricted to working within the household for security reasons. In other societies, girls are more likely to work as domestic servants because of the belief that it helps socialize them into gender-related adult roles, specifically as house-keepers. According to my research, parents and families are not permissive of child domestic servitude because of security reasons. Additionally, I understood that it is rather expectations of gender-related socialization on the part of both parents and the domestic servants themselves that drive parents to allow domestic servitude. As indicated in Chapter Six, parents and children believe that the domestic servant stands a chance of being exposed to city life, general etiquette, and training in decorum that they may not receive should they live in the villages their entire lives.

In reality, domestic servitude emerged in Ghana because of the quest for children to receive adequate gender socialization. The Director of Ghana's Social Welfare, Mrs. Mary Amadu, traced the history of domestic servitude in Ghana to the extended family's reliance on married female members to socialize younger members by training them in domestic chores, general comportment, and in some cases, providing them with formal education. An employer also told me that mothers from her hometown usually sent their teenage girls to live with her so she would be able to provide them with housekeeping training and to help them become independent adults and good wives.

Closely related to gender socialization is the impact of lineage on child domestic servitude. Using available literature, this research traced domestic servitude to the role of women in both matrilineal and patrilineal ethnic groups in Ghana. It argued that contrary to assertions in the literature that patriarchy did not exist in many African countries until colonization, matrilineal and patrilineal structures thrust much more economic and political power on men than women. Consequently, contemporary socialization in Ghana focuses on placing women in gender-related roles. Therefore, when families are not able to finance their young females through junior secondary schools, looking for households that they can serve and be able to eventually learn trades and household chores seem to be plausible options.

In regard to contemporary child slavery, this research could not find any compelling evidence that helps to categorize all of Ghana's domestic servants either as absolute slaves or free labor. The literature does not define the contemporary slave as persons who are owned as commodities. Rather, it is the nature of exploitation of the victims' labor, the age at which they are employed, their ability to consent to their employment and/or to voluntarily exit from it, and if they are paid at all. Processes of recruitment of the domestic servants who participated in this research were not enslaving. Kathleen Barry's (1984) convincing argument about the role of maturity and knowledgeability in children's ability to give consent to their employment led this research to the conclusion that most of the domestic servants are not absolute slaves in the contemporary sense. In the first place, a majority of my respondents were old enough to give consent to their employment. Additionally, they had received the basic education, and so I could not conclude that their rights of basic education had been violated. I could not define those who had dropped out of school as slaves either because at the time of their employment they were knowledgeable enough to even look for employers for themselves. They were not coerced into dropping out of school and into domestic servitude. Where the domestic servants could not voluntarily leave their employers' households, I observed that this was due to their parents' insistence on their remaining in domestic servitude until they received enough money to start learning trades.

I could define two of the current domestic servants as child domestic slaves using the criteria above, as they were too young to consent to their employment. I noted from the interviews that they would like to go back to their parents, but they did not have the freedom to do so. One of them, Selasie, did not know her parents or where she came from. The other young servant, Serena, knew her parents, but could not identify their place of residence. Neither of these two girls was given the chance to go to school. Besides long hours of unpaid services, they suffer all forms of abuses. Indisputably, Selasie and Serena are examples of contemporary slaves.

Although I could not categorize a majority of the respondents as contemporary slaves, the domestic servants, their parents, officials that I spoke to, the recruiters, and some employers admitted that the treatment that most of them receive from their employers is enslaving. They work under exploitative conditions that are slavery-like. If the majority of my respondents could neither be categorized as contemporary slaves nor free labor, how then can we identify and categorize them?

On one hand, we observe that most of these young women or girls have obtained the compulsory basic education or are old enough to qualify for employment within the household. They freely offer themselves for employment and, given their age and background, are at least knowledgeable, if not mature enough, to give informed consent about their recruitment. Some of them are able to learn trades and to become economically independent through domestic servitude. For these reasons, I have already pointed out that I could not categorize all of them as contemporary slaves. On the other hand, however, they work long hours, at times without pay, and, as most of them asserted, are treated as slaves. Given the domestic servants' willingness to stay as long as it takes to realize their dream of being enrolled in an apprenticeship, employers do not make good their part of the bargain by paying them off at the end of the agreed period. Based on these assertions, I could not discard their statuses as slaves; however, trivializing critics of the discourse on contemporary slavery might consider it.

This research defines Ghana's child domestic servitude as a form of labor-repressive system in which girls and young adults are exploited under slavery conditions. I differentiate them from the severely exploited and controlled contemporary slave by defining them as quasi-slaves. The level of exploitation that they suffer—and their own admittance as well as that of some of their parents, employers, the two government officials that I spoke to and their recruiters—could not be ignored. They are victims of labor-repressive systems as identified by Moore. To conclude, I have defined the quasi-slaves of Ghana's domestic servitude as persons who, although obtained through what might be described as acceptable means of recruitment, suffer verbal and physical abuses, stand a high probability of not being able to leave servitude for fear of losing their accrued incomes or for the lack of the freedom to do so, and who generally suffer forms of slavery-like exploitations and abuses.

TOWARDS THE ELIMINATION OF THE LABOR-REPRESSIVE SYSTEM OF CHILD DOMESTIC SERVITUDE IN GHANA: RECOMMENDATIONS

Ghana has ratified the three most important conventions that have been enforced to protect children and to eliminate worst forms of child labor exploitation. These are the ILO Convention concerning the Minimum Age for Admission to Employment (C138), the UN Convention on the Rights of the Child, and Convention on the Elimination of Worst Forms of Child Labor (C182). As the preceding chapters, especially Chapter Two illustrate, Ghana has embarked on many activities to protect its women and children. Unfortunately, these have not been successful. In this last section of this research, I submit recommendations that could advance the implementation of existing programs and thus help to eliminate child labor exploitation, or at least help reduce its prevalence.

This research illustrated the correlation between formal school participation and the incidence of child domestic servitude. It concluded that children who are never enrolled or drop out of school are most vulnerable to labor exploitation. Therefore, to effectively reduce or eliminate child labor exploitation, the first step would be to encourage school participation and retention. I outline a number of ways to motivate the children to remain in school. The provision of meals to school children during breaks is the first important step. This will reduce dependency on parents and compel them to ensure that their children attend school regularly. I assume that the children will also find a reason to be there. This would be costly to the government. An attempt on the part of the government to pass this cost onto parents would negate the very purpose of this plan as parents would prefer their children stay at home.

The above conclusions lead me to the second strategy of increasing participation in formal education in Ghana: the reduction in educational costs to parents. So far, the FCUBE has not worked. Under the FCUBE project, basic education in Ghana is supposed to be free. Nevertheless, new charges such as furniture fees, building fund, and Parent Teacher Association (PTA) dues (in addition to costs of stationery and books) make elementary education very expensive for rural and poor parents in general. Therefore, to ensure the success of the FCUBE, the Ghana government must honor its promise to make basic education free and compulsory by adequately providing the necessary resources. This gesture of official generosity is certainly indispensable for the attainment of the main objective of the FCUBE. The need for individual school administrators to levy various charges to parents must inevitably be eliminated. It might become crucial to criminalize such means of obtaining money from the poor.

In addition, instead of leaving the burden of the training of female drop-outs to employers and parents, a short-term program of sponsoring training could be instituted. This is the third strategy to solve the problem of child labor exploitation. This way, rural children will not consider domestic servitude as an indispensable approach through which they would become economically independent in adulthood. The implementation of such a short term program could also be adopted by domestic and international non-governmental organizations that have made the rights, welfare, and education of children important parts of their goals.

The fourth strategy is in regards to the training programs. In the long term, the training of girls to become hairdressers or dressmakers could be integrated into the regular curriculum of basic educational structures. I am aware that at the elementary school, children learn some basic sewing. Beyond elementary school training in dressmaking and hairdressing, parents who can afford it send their children to vocational schools for more advanced training. If the concentration of this training in basic schools is greater, it may not be so costly for graduates of junior secondary schools to continue their training and advance their skills to a higher level.

The above suggestions notwithstanding, I do not recommend an emphasis of the training of girls in hairdressing and dressmaking. This is in view of the anticipation that the market for hairdressers and dressmakers will be saturated soon given the rate at which graduates of Ghana's junior secondary schools enter these trades. Girls do not always have to be socialized into these low-paying-gender-biased occupations. As a result, I suggest that rural girls be made aware of other occupational choices and be provided the opportunity to train in them. When they are knowledgeable of the many occupational training opportunities that exist in training and education, both parents and children will strive to access and utilize them. In some rural communities where 60% of children coming out of the junior secondary schools do not acquire basic literacy and numeracy skills, both parents and children may lose sight of the significance of education if they are not persistently kept informed about schooling.

The fifth suggestion focuses on the government's attitude towards international conventions. Ghana was the first to accede to the CRC while more than half of those countries that first ratified it were African. However, it took ten years for 15 African countries to ratify the African Charter on the Rights and Welfare of the Child (ACRWC), which was adopted by the Organization of African Unity (OAU) in 1990 but came into force in 2000 (de Waal, 2002). Like Alex de Waal (2002), I wonder if signing international conventions is merely a symbolic act and an approach to acquiring status within the international community rather than a practical sign of commitment to solving the problems they purport to address.

Given the above, the government of Ghana must set in motion the criminalization of the use of non-school going children in domestic servitude. More importantly, stipulations in the many conventions that it has ratified must be implemented. This could be a hurdle for the government because many officials are guilty of using unpaid or underpaid domestic servants in their households. I, therefore, predict that it will take a well-informed public or grassroots movement to fight this canker. Rural children must be made aware of their rights. They must be educated on the CRC, the Children's Act of 1998, and the ACRWC. Abridged versions of these conventions and acts must be made available in local languages so that parents can understand them and make them a part of their traditional socialization processes. While I do not suggest the suppression of the Ghanaian child's understanding and acceptance of the obedience and respect for every adult, I believe that understanding their rights would help them distinguish between fear and respect and thus enable them to challenge and renounce abusive adults, be they relatives or employers. Additionally, being well informed would prepare them to hold officials accountable, bridging the gap between the realities of the Ghanaian child's vulnerability and the stipulations of the laws. As I stated earlier, children cannot go to court when they are abused. However, they can take advantage of WAJU and the Department of Social Welfare Services when they understand the instruments already in place to protect them.

Finally, the above proposals put forth will not materialize if corruption is not reduced. The government of Ghana has to implement realistic strategies that will reduce corruption while increasing accountability, especially among school administrators and government officials in general. If funding that could be put to use for the benefit of all is squandered by a few officials, the burden of educational funding on parents will likely remain high. Consequently, educational participation among the rural poor will continue to dwindle, and child labor exploitation will remain on the ascendance.

BIBLIOGRAPHY

Adepoju, A. & Oppong C. (1994). Gender, Work & Population in sub-Saharan Africa. London: James Currey for International Labour Office.

Allman, J.; Geiger, S. and Musisi, N. (Eds.) (2002). Women in African Colonial Histories. Indiana: Indiana University Press.

Anderson, B. (2004). Migrant domestic workers and slavery. In The Political Economy of the New Slavery. Hampshire: Palgrave Macmillan Ltd.

Anker, C. (2003). The Political Economy of the New Slavery. Hampshire: Palgrave Macmillan Ltd.

Archer, L. J. (ed.). (1988). Slavery and Other Forms of Unfree Labor. New York: Routledge.

Argenti, N. (2002). Youth in Africa, a major resource for change. In Alex de Waal and Nicolas Argenti (Eds.) (2002). Young Africa: Realizing The Rights of Children and Youth. Trenton: Africa World Press, Inc.

Aryee, A. F., (1997). The African family and changing nuptiality patterns. In Aderanti Adepuji (ed) Family, Population and Development in Africa. London: Zed Press.

Bales, K. (2000). New Slavery. California: ABC-CLIO, Inc.

Bales, K. (1999). Disposable People: New Slavery in the Global Economy. California: University of California Press.

Banpasirichote, C. (2000). Rapid economic growth: the social exclusion of children in Thailand. In The Exploited Child, Schlemmer, B. (Ed.). New York: Zed Books.

Berlan, A. (2004). Child labour, education and child rights among cocoa producers in Ghana. In The Political Economy of the New Slavery. Hampshire: Palgrave Macmillan Ltd.

Bonnet, M. (2000). Introduction: child labour in the light of bonded labour. In The Exploited Child, Schlemmer, B. (Ed.). New York: Zed Books.

Barry, K. (1984). Female Sexual Slavery. New York: New York University Press.

Bee, E. (1998). The Other Side of the Kitchen Door: Domestic Service in Lima, Peru. M.A. thesis, Department of Sociology and Anthropology, Florida International University, Miami.

Blagbrough, J & Glynn, E. (1999). Child domestic workers: characteristics of the modern slave and approaches to ending such exploitation. Childhood, 6 (1).

Burra, N. (1995). Born to Work: Child Labour in India. Delhi: Oxford University Press.

Cabanes, R. (2000). Family versus the logic of the market. In The Exploited Child, Schlemmer, B. (ed). New York: Zed Books.

Cadet, Jean-Robert (1998). Restavec: from Haitian Slaver Child to Middle-Class American. Texas: University of Texas Press.

Child Labor Coalition (2005). Child labor in the US: an overview of child labor laws. <http://www.stopchildlabor.org/USchildlabor/fact1.htm> Downloaded January 10, 2005)

Child labor on the increase. (1996) African Business, 6.

Coquery-Vidrovitch, C. (1997). African Women: A Modern History. Colorado: Westview Press.

Cox, K. E. (1999). The inevitability of nimble fingers? Law, development, and child labor. Vanderbilt Journal of Transnational Law, 32 (1), 115(1).

Derby, C. N. (2003). Conceptual Framework for Understanding Contemporary Child Slavery. M.A. Thesis, Department of Sociology and Anthropology, Florida International University, Miami.

Donkor, N. T. (2001). Impact of Structural Adjustment Policies on Forests and Natural Resource Management. In Konadu-Agyemang, K. (2001). IMF and World Bank Sponsored Structural Adjustment Programs in Africa: Ghana's Experiences, 1983-1999. USA: Ashgate Publishing Limited.

Donkor, K. (1997). Structural Adjustment and Mass Poverty in Ghana. Aldershot: Ashgate Publishing Ltd.

Ellis, F. (1998). Household strategies and rural livelihood diversification. Journal of Development Studies, 35 (1), 1-38.

France, D. (2000). Slavery's new face. Newsweek, 118 (6255), 84-89.

Fukui, L. (2000) Why is child labour tolerated? The case of Brazil. In The Exploited Child, Schlemmer, B. (Ed.). New York: Zed Books.

Gendreau, F. (2000) Public policy, society and child labour. In The Exploited Child, Schlemmer, B. (Ed.). New York: Zed Books.

The Ghanaian Chronicle. (2004). MPS Plead: Grace Coleman Deserves a Second Chance. <http://www.ghanaian-chronicle.com/thestory.asp?ID=64>. (Downloaded August 20, 2004).

Ghana Home Page. (2004). General Information. http://www.ghanaweb.com/ GhanaHomePage/general/. (Downloaded May 24, 2004).

Ghanaweb.com. (2002) Indictment of Grace Coleman. http://www.ghanaweb.com/ GhanaHomePage/NewsArchive/artikel.php?ID=41836. (Downloaded May 25, 2004).

Gladwin, C. (ed). (1991). Structural Adjustment and African Women. Florida: University of Florida Press.

Goheen, M. (1991). The ideology and political economy of gender: women and land in Nso, Cameroon. In Gladwin C. (Ed.). (1991). Structural Adjustment and African Women. Florida: University of Florida Press.

Guyer, J. I. (1984). Women in the economy: contemporary variations. In Hay, M J. and Stichter S. (eds). (1984). African Women South of the Sahara. New York: Longman Inc.

Hawkins, S. (2002). "The Woman in Question": Marriage and Identity in the Colonial Courts of Northern Ghana, 1907-1954. In Allman, J.; Geiger, S. and Musisi, N. (Eds.) (2002). Women in African Colonial Histories. Indiana: Indiana University Press: 116-143.

Henn, J. K. (1984). Women in the rural economy: past, present, and past. In Hay, M J. and Stichter S. (eds). (1984). African Women South of the Sahara. New York: Longman Inc.

Hormeku, T. (1997). Ghana: the Numbers of the Last Five Years. <http://www.socwatch.org.uy/1997/ghana.htm> Downloaded August 21 2003)

Hondagneu-Sotelo, P. (2001). Domestica: Immigrant Workers Cleaning and Caring in the Shadows of Affluence. California: University of California Press.

Human Rights Watch Children's Right Project (1996). The Small Hands of Slavery: Bonded Child Labor in India. New York: Human rights Watch.

Innocenti Research Center (Undated). Data Base on Child Labour in India: An Assessment with Respect to Nature of Data, Period and Uses. India: Thorat, S.

Innocenti Research Center (2002). Child Work in Cote d'Ivoire. India: Francavilla, G., Lyon, S.

Innocenti Research Centre (1999). Child domestic work. Innocenti Digest, 5.

ILO – International Programme on the Elimination of Child Labour (2002). Thailand - Child Domestic Workers: A Rapid Assessment. Geneva: Phlainoi, N.

International Labor Organization. (2001a). Stopping Forced Labor: Global Report under the Follow-up to the ILO Fundamental Principles and Rights at Work. Geneva: International Labor Office.

International Labor Organization. (2001b). Nepal Situation of Domestic Child Laborers in Kathmandu: A Rapid Assessment. Geneva: Sharma, S; Thakurathi, M; Sapkota, K.; Devkota, B.; and Rimal, B.

International Labor Organization (2002a). IPEC Action against Child Labor: Progress and Future Priorities. Geneva: International Labor Organization.

International Labor Organization. (2002b). Tanzania - Child Labour in the Informal Sector: A Rapid Assessment. Geneva: Kadonya C., Madihi M., Mtwana, S.

International Labor Organization and Inter-Parliamentary Union. (2002). Eliminating the Worst Forms of Child Labor: A Practical Guide to ILO Convention 182. Geneva: ILO.

Kasper, A. (1994). "A feminist, qualitative methodology: a study of women with breast cancer". Qualitative Sociology, 17 (3), 263-281.

Kevane, M. (2004). Women and Development in Africa. Colorado: Lynne Rienner Publishers, Inc.

Kimaryo, M. and Pouwels, R. (1999). An African perspective: Child domestic workers in Tanzania. Child Workers in Asia 15 (2), 26-28.

Konadu-Agyemang K. and Takyi, B. K. (2001) Structural Adjustment Programs and the Political Economy of Development and Underdevelopment in Ghana. In Konadu-Agyemang K. (2001). IMF and World Bank Sponsored Structural Adjustment Programs in Africa: Ghana's Experiences, 1983-1999. USA: Ashgate Publishing Limited.

Kopytoff, I. (1986). The cultural biography of things: commoditization as process. In Appadurai A (ed) (1986). The Social Life of Things: Commodities in Cultural Perspective. United Kingdom: Cambridge University Press.

Landsdown, G. (1994). Children's Rights. In Children's Childhoods Observed and Experienced, Mayall, B. (Ed.) (1994). London: The Falmer Press

Lange, M. (2000). The demand for labour within the household: child labour in Togo. In The Exploited Child, Schlemmer, B. (Ed.). New York: Zed Books.

Lukas E. (1996). Saving the Children. National Review, 48 (24) 30-31.

Marguerat, Y. (2000). The exploitation of apprentices in Togo. In The Exploited Child, Schlemmer, B. (ed). New York: Zed Books.

Mbaye S. M. and Fall, S. A. (2000). The disintegrating social fabric: child labour and socialization in Senegal. In The Exploited Child, Schlemmer, B. (Ed.). New York: Zed Books.

Mbembe, A. (2001). On the Postcolony. California: University of California Press

Meert, H; Mistiaen, P.& Kesteloot, C. (1997). The geography of survival: household strategies in urban setting. Tijdschrift Voor Economische en Sociale Geografie, 88, 169-181.

Meillassoux, C. (2000). The economy and child labour: an overview. In The Exploited Child, Schlemmer, B. (Ed.). New York: Zed Books.

Meltzer, M. (1980). All times, All Peoples: A World History of Slavery. New York: Harper & Row, Publishers.

Mikell, G. (Ed.). (1997). African Feminism: the Politics of Survival in Sub-Saharan Africa. Pennsylvania: University of Pennsylvania Press.

Mishra, L. (2000). Child Labour in India. New York: Oxford University Press.

Mikay, E. (1997). An economic essential? The Middle East, 272, 38-40.

Moore, B. Jr. (1966). Social Origins of Dictatorship and Democracy: Lord and Peasant in the Making of the Modern World. Massachusetts: Beacon Press.

Morice, A. (2000). Paternal domination: the typical relationship conditioning the exploitation of children. In The Exploited Child, Schlemmer, B. (Ed.). New York: Zed Books.

Martin, G. (2002). Africa in World Politics. New Jersey: Africa World Press.

Nukunya, G. K. (1992). Tradition and Change in Ghana: an Introduction to Sociology. Accra: Ghana Universities Press.

Obbo, C. (1980). African Women: Their Struggle for Economic Independence. London: Zed Press.

Oppong, C. (1974) Marriage among a Matrilineal Elite: a Family Study of Ghanaian Senior Civil Servants. London: Cambridge University Press.

Owusu, F. (2001). Urban Impoverishment and Multiple Modes of Livelihood in Ghana. Ph.D.Dissertation, Department of Community and Regional Planning, Iowa State University, Ames.

Oyewumi, O. (1997). The Invention of Women: Making an African Sense of Western Gender Discourse. Minneapolis: University of Minnesota Press.

Palmie, S. (Ed.). (1995). Slave Cultures and the Cultures of Slavery. Knoxville: The University of Tennessee Press.

Patterson, O. (1982). Slavery and Social Death: a comparative study. Massachusettes: Harvard University Press.

Ramanathan, U. (2000). The public policy problem: child labour and the law in India. In The Exploited Child, Schlemmer, B. (Ed.). New York: Zed Books.

Ravololomanga, B. and Sclermer, B. (2000). 'Unexploited" labour: social transition in Madagascar. In The Exploited Child, Schlemmer, B. (Ed.). New York: Zed Books.

Reh, M. and Ludwar-Ene, G. (Eds.). (1995). Gender Identity in Africa. Munster: Lit.

Robertson, C. C. (184). Women in the urban economy. In Hay, M J. and Stichter S. (eds). (1984). African Women South of the Sahara. New York: Longman Inc.

Robson, E. (1996). Working girls and boys: children's contributions to household survival in West Africa. Geography, 81 (4), 403(5).

Romm, N. and Rwomire, A. (2001). Child abuse: the sociological perspective. In Rwomire, A. (ed). African women and Children. (2001). Connecticut: Praeger Publishers.

Rone, J. (1995). Children in Sudan: Slaves, street Children and Child Soldiers. New York: Human Rights Watch.

Sawyer, R. (1988). Childhood Enslaved. London: Routledge.

Schlemmer, B. (Ed.). (2000). The Exploited Child. New York: Zed Books.

Seabrook, J. (2000). Child workers, the shifting debate. Race and Class, 42 (2), 80.

Shoishab. (1997). Child domestics in Dhaka, Bangladesh. Child Workers in Asia, 13 (1), 4-6

Slater, W. (1997). Are any domestic helpers employed in your household? Child Workers in Asia, 13 (1), 26-27.

SLIMG Sri Lanka. (1997). Live-in servants in Sri Lanka. Child Workers in Asia, 13 (1), 14-16.

Stark, O. (1991), The Migration of Labor. Cambridge: Basil Blackwell.

Stahl, A. and Cruz, M. D. (1998). Men and women in a market economy: gender and craft production in West Central Ghana, ca. 1775-1995. In Kent, S. (Ed.). (1998). Gender in African Prehistory. London: Altamira Press.

Stoeltje, B.J. (1995). Asante queenmothers: a study. In Reh, M. and Ludwar-Ene, G. (Eds.). (1995). Gender Identity in Africa. Munster: Lit

Sunoo, B. P. (2000). Caution: children at work. Workforce, 79 (9), 44.

Tashjian, V. B. and Allman, J. (2002). Marrying and Marrying on a Shifting Terrain: Reconfigurations of Power and Authority in Early Colonial Asante. In Allman, J.; Geiger, S. and Musisi, N. (Eds.) (2002). Women in African Colonial Histories. Indiana: Indiana University Press: 237-259

Tucker L. and Ganesan, A. (1997). The small hands of slavery: India's bonded child laborers and the World Bank. Multinational Monitor, 18 (1-2), 17-19.

UNICEF. (1999). Child domestic work. The Innocenti Digest. Florence: International Child Development Center.

UNICEF. (1998). Girls at work. New York: UNICEF.

United Nations Commission on Human Rights, (2002). The relationship between child domestic servitude and the sexual exploitation of children. <http://www.antislavery.org/archive/submission/submission2002-childlabour.htm>.

US Justice Department. (2004). Maryland Couple Sentenced for Forced Labor. http://www.usdoj.gov/usao/md/press_releases/press04/BlackwellSent.pdf (Downloaded June, 2004)

Van Gennep, A. (1960). The Rites of Passage. Translated by Monika B. Vizedom and Gabrielle L. Caffee. Chicago: The University of Chicago Press.

Verlet, M. (2000). Growing up in Ghana: deregulation and the employment of children. In The Exploited Child, Schlemmer, B. (ed). New York: Zed Books.

Waal, A. de (2002). Realizing child rights in Africa children, young people and leadership. In Alex de Waal and Nicolas Argenti (Eds.) (2002). Young Africa: Realizing The Rights of Children and Youth. Trenton: Africa World Press, Inc.

White, L. (1984). Women in the changing African family. In Hay, M J. and Stichter S. (eds). (1984). African Women South of the Sahara. New York: Longman Inc.

The World Bank (2002) Upgrading of Low Income Settlements: Country Assessment Report. <http://www.worldbank.org/urban/upgrading/docs/afr-assess/ghana.pdf> (Downloaded August 31, 10, 2003).

The World Bank. (2004). Ghana at a Glance. <http://www.worldbank.org/data/countrydata/aag/gha_aag.pdf> Downloaded January 10, 2005).

INDEX

AUTHOR BIOGRAPHY

C. Nana Derby is an Assistant Professor of Criminal Justice at Virginia State University. She graduated from Florida International University with a Ph.D. in Comparative Sociology. Her research revolves around contemporary slavery, feminist criminology, and crimes of transnational migration. Her Ph.D. dissertation, which culminated in the publication of this book, investigated the use of children as domestic servants in some Ghanaian households. In the future, she plans to undertake a historical comparative research on gender, colonization, and the criminal justice system. She has published articles and has made several scholarly presentations on child labor exploitation and contemporary slavery.